RAISING WORLDY-WISE BUT INNOCENT KIDS

RAISING WORLDLY-WISE BUT INNOCENT KIDS

BY

DAVID WYRTZEN

MOODY PRESS
CHICAGO

130026

To my dad, Jack Wyrtzen,
who was my example of a wise father
on his knees before God each morning
with the sacred Scriptures,

and to my Hebrew teacher, Bruce Waltke,
who gave me not only exegetical tools
but the example of a life filled with passion—
passion to study the Hebrew text
and to bring it to life in the marketplace

Contents

Acknowledgments

My students at the Word of Life Bible Institute, my church family in Midlothian, Texas, and most of all my four children, Jonathan, Joel, Joshua, and Jenae, gave me the opportunity to see the power of the ancient text of Proverbs transform lives today. Without them this book would be lifeless. And without my faithful ally at my side this book could not have been written. Thanks, Mary, for your heart and your encouragement.

I am also indebted to Duncan Jaenicke and the staff of Moody Press who believed in the realistic Learn-and-Live philosophy of parenting and used their editorial and publishing skills to bring these principles into the lives of parents and their teenagers through the printed page.

Foreword

Many summers ago, my wife, Jill, and I were regular attenders at Word of Life Bible Camp at Schroon Lake, New York. We always looked forward to the outstanding weeks of Bible training and spiritual leadership we received there. It was during one of those summers that young David Wyrtzen crossed our path.

Our immediate response was that this young man could not teach us anything new. It soon became evident, however, that he had much to share from the book of Proverbs. Under his instruction, the ancient proverbs came alive. He breathed a new freshness into them and imparted a vitality and meaningfulness that we had never before experienced.

Jill and I used to wish that we could have all of the life applications from Proverbs in book form that we could use in our personal study and also share with our twelve kids. You can imagine how excited we were when we learned that Moody Press had agreed to publish Dave Wyrtzen's unique insights into Proverbs. Even more thrilling is Dave's unique, easily understood style as he applies the age-old principles to parenting today's fast-track kids.

I am delighted that Dave has written this practical, much-needed book. This kind of treatment is long overdue. After you finish reading this remarkable book, I'm sure you will agree with me that the book of Proverbs has never been more alive and more ably applied to the challenging task of raising our kids to face real life.

Three cheers for Dave Wyrtzen . . . and for King Solomon!

PAT WILLIAMS
General Manager, Orlando Magic, NBA
Co-author of the best-selling book *Rekindled*

9

Introduction

Parenting the Star Wars generation is intimidating. When I compete against my kids in Atari® or Nintendo®, I become painfully aware of this reality. It's humbling for me to lose to Joshua, my eight-year-old, in a video game. It's more humbling to realize that my sons and daughter are learning in elementary school things I learned in college. State-of-the-art media flashes everything before their eyes from Michael Jackson to the explosion of the space shuttle *Challenger*. The Star Wars generation has an air of technical sophistication, but does it have a clear grasp of spiritual realities or moral standards? Does our children's broadened exposure through media and quicker acceptance of new technology guarantee that they have a clear idea of how to live a skillful life?

The scandal of powerful preachers caught sleeping with prostitutes while moneyed Wall Street brokers go to jail for acting illegally on inside information and magazine headlines that read "What Ever Happened to Ethics—Assaulted by sleaze, scandals and hypocrisy, America searches for its moral bearings" (*Time*, May 25, 1987) suggest that computer chips are not giving young people or adults the right moral programs.

As a dad, I feel an intense desire to protect my kids from all the immorality, deception, substance abuse, and violence of contemporary America. Sometimes I dream of isolating them in a monastery where they would be safe from the seduction of evil.

THE MONASTERY PARENT

As I counsel, I find many parents who identify with my feelings of wanting to isolate our kids from the influence of the secular world. I refer to this philosophy of raising kids as "monastery parenting." Fred and Mary represent this approach.

In their college days during the sixties they experimented with drugs and "free love" life-styles. In the midst of their search for meaning, a friend challenged them to consider the Person of Jesus Christ. After reading the gospel of John, they both opened their lives to Him. Their pasts make them painfully aware of the power of evil, and they know the scars sin can cause. They fear for their ten- and eight-year-olds. Over coffee in their living room Fred shares his concerns.

"I thought things were coming apart in the sixties, but things have deteriorated even more today. Last night Lance asked me if they had 'crack' when I was growing up. And last Friday he brought home a piece of paper covered with occult pentagrams. One of his classmates told him they were nice designs. I fear for my kids, and I intend to protect my family by creating a Christian environment. The rules concerning dress, music, and entertainment will be strict. I'll make sure they never come into contact with the influences that seduced me. I'm going to build a wall around my children which will guarantee that no corrupting influences can pollute their innocent minds."

I empathize with Fred and Mary's concern, but I question their "ignorance is bliss" solution. Will turning back the clock to the days of "Father Knows Best" and "Leave It to Beaver" conquer evil's internal and external blitz against our kids?

Too often I hear the cries of monastery parents *after* the reality of evil has scaled their protective walls:

"We attended a gospel-preaching, Bible-teaching church, but now our fifteen-year-old is pregnant."

"Our kids were never allowed to touch a drop! How could our John be expelled from school for having beer on the campus?"

"We sent Debbie to a good Christian college. How could she be so cold concerning spiritual things now that she has graduated?"

"Our pastor exhorted against perversion each Sunday. How could he have been having affairs with so many women?"

Nostalgic reruns from the fifties will not equip us or our children to face the sophisticated temptations of the nineties. We cannot turn back the clock. Ecclesiastes 7:10 warns us against yearning for the good old days: "Do not say, 'Why were the old days better than these?' It is not wise to ask such questions."

In reality, the monastery approach was thoroughly tested in the "good old days." It failed!

The first-century Pharisees were Super Bowl champions at trying to conquer temptation by isolationism and rigid rules. They critically attacked Jesus because His disciples did not honor the traditions passed down by their learned religious teachers (Mark 7:5)—traditions skillfully designed to erect a wall around the moral law of God so human passions could be controlled and the individual protected from yielding to evil.

Jesus' reply to these religionists reveals the internal inconsistency whenever any of us tries to generate morality by locking people into an external behavior pattern. The monastery approach fails because it attempts to clean up internal, moral filth with an external bath.

> Isaiah was right when he prophesied about you hypocrites; as it is written: "These people honor me with their lips, but their hearts are far from me. They worship me in vain; their teachings are but rules taught by men."
>
> (Mark 7:6-7; NIV*)

The monastery philosophy of raising children cannot generate a deep intimacy with God, which alone yields a wise and moral lifestyle. It mislocates the problem of evil in external influences rather than in internal conditions. Walls cannot be built high enough to keep evil away from our kids. It has already infected their internal nature from the beginning. The isolationist technique is an impotent religious tradition that can never check the virility of evil. Jesus labeled this legalism *stupidity*!

New International Version.

Are you so dull? Don't you see that nothing that enters a man from the outside can make him "unclean"? . . . For from within, out of men's hearts, come evil thoughts, sexual immorality, theft, murder, adultery, greed, malice, deceit, lewdness, envy, slander, arrogance and folly. All these things come from inside and make a man "unclean."

(Mark 7:18, 21-23; NIV)

Jesus discerned the weakness of the monastery approach: it mislocates the enemy and is powerless to turn a rebel into a trusting child of God.

Children raised in monastery-style environments—where devotion to God is equivalent to attending church services, giving a few coins in the offering, memorizing Bible verses, and having the correct haircut—tend to grow up and flee those restrictions. Regretfully, they often rebel against the spiritual values of their parents and experiment with evil. When they marry and have children, they often vow there will be no rigid rules in their home. Their children will be free to discover their own standards. Thus, in reaction to rigidity, the pendulum swings to the opposite extreme—the laissez-faire approach.

THE LAIZZEZ-FAIRE PARENT

Laissez-faire is a philosophy that deliberately abstains from giving direction. Its adherents focus on noninterference and stress individual freedom of choice and action. When applied to parenting it means refraining from inhibiting a child's creative self-development. The laissez-faire parent chooses not to give authoritative guidance in spiritual or moral matters.

Charlene's dad is the pastor of a large fundamentalist church. In her teen years she rebelled, ran away from home, and got pregnant. A one-year marriage to the father of her child proved to be disaster. Now at twenty-eight she is married to a successful attorney, and her career in interior design has taken off. During a quick lunch between appointments she shares some of her thoughts about raising her kids.

"Patrick and I trust our children. We want them to experiment and follow their instincts. Why not let them have their flings? After all, in spite of my dad's multitude of sermons, I sowed my wild oats. All that church attendance and Bible-reading my parents subjected me to didn't keep me from getting into trouble. My children will have the right to discover their own personal meaning without my interference. At least they are not growing up in all that pious hypocrisy."

I asked Charlene if I could share a challenge my wife and I faced in teaching our three-year-old daughter, Jenae, the meaning of the word *hot*. She nodded.

"We use a wood burning stove to heat our home. When cranked up, its surface temperature peaks at about one thousand degrees Fahrenheit. One day Mary came to me with concern, 'Dave, if Jenae plants her little palm on that stove, she will be scarred for life!'

"My masculine laissez-faire response was, 'That would teach her! She'd never touch hot stoves again.'"

I asked Charlene what kind of parent she would consider me to be if I allowed Jenae to learn about hot stoves through trial and error experimentation? She grimaced at the thought of Jenae's charred palm.

The laissez-faire parent forgets that the school of experience is efficient but cruel. A grotesquely scarred palm is too high a price to pay to learn the meaning of the word *hot*. The multiple deaths of teenagers is too high a cost to learn that the illicit use of drugs is wrong. Becoming the victim of AIDS or giving birth to an illegitimate baby is too high a price for a lesson in the advantages of sexual purity. The learn-by-experience, do-your-own-thing approach was popular in the sixties, but in the nineties we must wise up to its wreckage of human lives. So where do we go from here? What is an effective parental training model for the final decade of the twentieth century? How should our children learn about the "hot spots" in life?

LEARN-AND-LIVE PARENTING

When Mary confronted me with the danger posed by our stove, I immediately contacted a skilled welder. He built a large, metal screen around the stove so that Jenae could not get near the

searing surface. We then began an intense course in the meaning of
hot. I took her by the hand and brought her near the stove where she
could feel the heat. "Hot! Hot!" We repeated, "Hurt, Jenae! Ow!
Don't touch!"

This approach depends upon our genuine love for her as our
daughter, our personal conviction concerning the danger of hot
stoves, and our effectiveness in teaching her those two realities. Effective training can bring her to the day when she will no longer
need the screen. Jenae can mature to the point that she will decide
for herself that it is foolish to get burned by insisting on planting her
fist on a hot stove. She may choose to learn this lesson by getting
burned. But she will be way ahead if she accepts our love and the
reality of our teaching concerning the pain of burned flesh.

Today's generation needs adults who will love them enough to
point out the hot spots in life, build authoritative fences to protect
them from these dangers while they are immature, and invest the
personal time necessary to train teenagers to make right ethical
choices on their own. Our lives must demonstrate the happiness
found in living wisely. We must stop coveting our teenagers' youth
and fully accept our adult responsibility to teach the next generation
how to live. But where do we find the correct principles for living?

Though dusty with age and far removed from the *New York
Times* best-seller list, the Old Testament book of Proverbs is still the
ultimate parental training manual. These proverbs may appear to be
quaint, old-fashioned relics of a bygone era or obvious trivialities
that everyone should know. But when mined with perseverance,
they become nuggets that glisten with life's realities.

Proverbs is a gutsy book about money, sex, and power. It exposes the con-game of the drug pusher, the seduction of the prostitute, and the sarcasm of the agnostic university professor. It does
not blush when talking about the intimacies of sexual love or shrink
from the evolutionist's challenge concerning the creation. Its greatest gift? The revelation of God's personal philosophy of child-rais-
ing.

God chooses neither the protectionism of the monastery nor
the experimentation of the laissez-faire method. Instead, He penetrates deep inside our children's personalities and challenges them
with the choices in life that bring success and those that yield disas-

ter. He courts them to choose to love, trust, and respect Him. He advises them to be worldly-wise but to remain innocent—wise as a serpent concerning evil's allure but pure as a dove concerning involvement in sin. His top priority is an invitation. He desires to live inside their personalities and give them the power to not only know but also to make the right choice.

Will our children be able to say that their dad and mom loved them enough to teach them not just how to make a living but how to live? When our children leave the shelter of our homes, will they be sheltered by the wisdom that only God can teach?

These are not only theoretical issues for me. Mary and I are in the midst of raising three sons and a daughter. Just yesterday, it seems, I waited nervously in the waiting room—back when dads were not welcome in the delivery room—while Mary gave birth to our oldest. Today he is asking me to teach him to drive. Tomorrow we'll be checking out colleges, and the next day he'll be on his own. Our parenting days are moving at the speed of light. Will we use these speeding moments to train Jonathan, Joel, Joshua, and Jenae in God's school of skillful living? Or will they be left to the school of hard knocks? Time and the personal decisions our children make will answer this question. What about your kids?

My purpose in writing is to share the facts about life God is teaching me from Proverbs, to share how my family is struggling to apply the learn-and-live approach to parenting in the computer age, to learn together how to avoid sending our kids to the school of hard knocks. Our first task is to find a "Dr. Spock" who will tell us the truth about raising kids—someone whose advice will not become obsolete when the next best seller tops the charts.

THINK ABOUT IT

1. When you send your kids away to a college or a career, what objectives do you hope to have accomplished in their lives? Write these objectives down, and discuss them with your spouse and kids.

2. How did your parents impart values to you? Where did they succeed? Where did they fail? How is your parental pattern a reaction to your upbringing?

3. What is the dominant parental philosophy of your home? Monastery approach? Laissez-faire? Learn-and-live? How do you as husband and wife differ in philosophy?

4. Think of a situation in which you as parents did train one of your children in a life reality, with the goal of helping him or her become skillful in making such decisions alone. How did your child respond? Why is the learn-and-live approach difficult?

The Designer:
A Father with a Skillful Plan
for Living

Intimacy with the Creator
is the greatest gift we can give our children.

1

A Wise Head on Young Shoulders

"Super catch, Gary! Trying to tackle me?"

The senior wide receiver was relieved that Cathy, one of the cheerleaders, could still talk. He had managed to hold on to the football but had knocked her flat when he fell out of bounds.

"Sorry! You OK, Cathy? Their defensive cornerback tried to plant me in the stands. I'll tell our quarterback to stay away from the sideline pass, but at least I made the catch and a first down!"

"Cheerleading gets dangerous at times." She laughed.

Gary returned to join his team in the huddle but not before he took another glance toward the sideline. Cathy's smile, blonde hair to her waist, and slim figure could turn any football player's head.

A spectator glancing at these two East Texas High School teenagers could easily conclude that their lives would have charmed destinies. Physically attractive, intellectually gifted, socially desirable—success? They couldn't miss! Graduation day that spring thrust these seniors upon the serious path of adult life—a path that took them to completely different destinations. Only one of them was prepared for the trip.

Cathy decided she needed some practical exposure to the nine-to-five world of business before furthering her education. The Dallas-Fort Worth Metroplex invited her to the land of opportunity. Her parents were reluctant, but when Susan, a longtime friend of the family, moved up to the Metroplex from Austin, Mom and Dad gave in. The new roommates moved into an apartment and made plans to take on the world.

Dressed smartly in her tailored suit, Cathy's "cover girl" look landed her a job in no time as a receptionist in North Dallas. The money was only fair, but the social life was magnificent. Susan tried to interest Cathy in a career class at a church near their apartment, but Cathy couldn't help thinking how boring the get-togethers were compared to the clubs Joan was introducing her to.

Joan was the boss's secretary. Sophisticated and fun, she knew the right clothes, night spots, and men. Cathy never dreamed life could be so fast and free.

"Jack Jones is doing the Venetian Room at the Fairmont Friday night, Cathy. I'll pick you up at your apartment at seven o'clock." Thirty, successful, and smooth, Mick Johnson was confident with women. Running into him in the hall after returning from a fifteen-minute coffee break caught Cathy by surprise, but she managed to blurt out, "Yes, Mick, that sounds like fun."

To a nineteen-year-old, Jack Jones was boring, but with Mick even a piano recital could be scintillating. Susan nagged her with questions about Mick's character. Cathy felt like she was living with her mother again instead of with an eighteen-year-old roommate.

The girls in the office teased her all week about her date with the new man in town. But in the soft, dim light of the Venetian Room Friday evening the men could not stop glancing at the petite girl in the romantic lace cocktail dress. Mick did not tease.

He refilled Cathy's wine glass and tenderly took her hand. He mentioned his hotel room quietly but with confidence. This was a far cry from the bumbling high school boys she had dated. The wine was sweet, and his touch was slow and reassuring. With Jack Jones's love ballads filling her mind, Cathy spent her first night in bed with a man.

Saturday morning when she returned to her apartment, Cathy felt dirty and used. Susan almost convinced her to go and talk to her pastor, but she overslept and missed morning worship. Monday at work Cathy finally spilled her feelings to Joan. Over lunch her friend knew how to soothe a troubled conscience.

"Do you think you're the only girl in the office who has lost her virginity? Don't worry about it. You just grew up a little."

Joan was right. Some of her friends in the office did enjoy this pleasure from time to time. There was some concern about AIDS, but, if precautions were taken, most believed there was little danger. Their lives didn't fall apart because of a little illicit sex.

Cathy was offered her first joint during her lunch break, and her first experience with cocaine came at a Saturday night pool party. She had never felt so lighthearted and confident—confident enough to keep dating Mick. An invitation to spend a weekend with him on his yacht in Galveston was the culmination of a series of exhilarating highs.

Cathy's parents heard nothing from their daughter for three years. The police tried to trace her, but the computer readout was still zero after a few months' investigation. Cathy's name became another statistic in the runaway file, but her parents kept praying and hoping.

Life-changing choices. My kids and your kids will have to make them on their own someday. Our parental responsibility is to prepare them for graduation day, for a safe solo flight. A monastery cannot shelter them, and the school of hard knocks (live and learn) might murder them. But, turning this around, the learn-and-live philosophy assumes that we know an expert on child development whom we can count on. Allow me to introduce a genuine expert. His insight into life was so sharp that some have called him the wisest man who ever lived.

THE BEN FRANKLIN OF ANCIENT ISRAEL

Who comes to mind when I mention the words *proverb* and *Poor Richard's Almanac*? For the American, it is Ben Franklin. In ancient Israel the name that epitomized proverbial teaching was not Franklin but Solomon. God titled His handbook for skillful parenting "The Proverbs of Solomon the Son of David, King of Israel" (Proverbs 1:1).

Talk about a man with experience! Solomon possessed greater political power than a United States president, more wealth than Texas oil baron J. R. Ewing, and more women than *Playboy's* Hugh Hefner. He spent most of his life experimenting with power, wealth, and sex in an attempt to discover what would yield lasting satisfaction. He learned about reality the hard way—by experience. So why is he the principal human author of Proverbs? Because he tried it all. He was an "A" student in the school of experience. He knew the facts of life firsthand. Therefore, if our children will listen to his instruction, they can learn from his example and avoid going to the school of hard knocks themselves.

In pithy, easy-to-remember maxims Solomon encapsulated the principles of skillful living that he gleaned from his own experience and from the collective experience of Israel and the surrounding Near Eastern kingdoms. He epitomized a wisdom movement in Israel that endured. Two hundred and fifty years after his death, scribes in the court of Hezekiah were not only composing their own wisdom sayings (Proverbs 22:17–24:34) but were also preserving the proverbs of Solomon (Proverbs 25:1). These wise men took their place along with the priest and the prophet as spiritual guides in Israel (Jeremiah 18:18). God inspired some of their advice concerning the training of the young and preserved it for us in the Old Testament book of Proverbs.

This divine instruction manual does not immediately plunge us into the difficult waters of understanding the 375 solomonic proverbs (10:1–22:16). Instead, a brief introduction (1:2-6) and motto (1:7) state the purpose of the book and its foundational principle. Then a lengthy exhortation from a wise dad and mom seeks to incite us to pay attention to what Solomon and the other wise men have to say (1:8–9:18).

These parents adopt a practical motivational technique: "Listen to what we tell you, and life will reward you. Reject our instructions, and you might not live to tell about it."

We cannot expect our children to eagerly accept this "preaching." They need to see wisdom fleshed out in our personal lives. We must not be like the parent who delivers a lecture on the risks of lung cancer while shaking another cigarette out of the box and asking for a light.

All of us know that what we are speaks so loudly our children are deaf to what we say. Solomon's life reiterated this truism. He had the right ideas in his head but not in his life. Rehoboam, Solomon's son (1 Kings 12), followed his dad's life, not his words. Rehoboam's foolish pride was deaf to good advice. He demolished the united kingdom his father and grandfather had given their lives to create (1 Kings 12:16-17).

Our children will also rebel against hypocrisy. They need to see a consistent life, not just right words. The purpose of Proverbs is to reveal how to do this—to internalize skillful living in our personal and family life.

A GOAL FOR PARENTS AND CHILDREN

Effective parenting is more than teaching facts about life or the Bible. Our kids might be champion Bible trivia players, but that does not guarantee they will have moral character. The memorization of biblical facts and verses is a beginning, but we must go on to ask what God is teaching about Himself, ourselves, and life. Our daily walk must illustrate how to apply biblical principles to the changing circumstances of real situations. If our children see genuine satisfaction in our lives resulting from the application of wisdom, they will desire to follow our example. The introduction to Proverbs states the goal for parents and children this way: "to know the art of skillful living which comes through disciplined training; to discern the words of insight" (Proverbs 1:2).

To internalize this purpose we must discern the exact meaning of three common words—knowledge, wisdom, and discipline.

KNOWLEDGE

When Hebrew sages spoke about "knowledge," they had far more in mind than filling in the right box on a multiple choice exam or getting 1600 on the SAT. A cassette recorder can out-perform humans at rote memory tests every time. True education begins with memorization but goes on to include the application of information in changing situations. A student may score high on a sex information exam in school, but can he resist an immoral person who is attempting to seduce him?

We need to think through these life situations with our children. They need us to explain the whys, not just give commands. The goal is more than obedience. They must learn to see past initial choices to their consequences and then commit themselves to behavior that will produce lasting satisfaction. In the school of wisdom the student does not pass until he knows how to respond in real-life situations. Practical values need to be knit into the fabric of their lives.

WISDOM

When the sage spoke of wisdom, he did not mean some ivory-tower, impractical ideal unrelated to life. To know wisdom meant to internalize moral and spiritual values deep within your personality, so you could skillfully apply them in concrete situations. The Hebrew term for wisdom was so practical that it was often used for the skill possessed by an expert craftsman or sailor.

When I was a teenager, my dad and mom took me on vacation to Nassau in the Caribbean. A small sailboat was tied to a pier, and the ocean challenged me to demonstrate my skills as a seaman, which I had learned on the treacherous lakes of upstate New York. I convinced Dad to go along too.

After tipping the craft over three times and almost drowning my father, it became obvious that I was not prepared to sail in four-foot surf. I was not a wise sailor. To make it in that bay, you needed more than book knowledge about the parts of a sailboat. You needed applied knowledge about sails, wind, currents, and the proper handling of a small craft in difficult seas. The owner of the boat did possess this skill, and I enjoyed several safe sails with her.

Wisdom in Proverbs is the ability to sail safely through the difficult seas of life. The only way to obtain this skill is through disciplined training and practice under the tutelage of a mature teacher.

DISCIPLINE

If one is studying a trade, a sport, or music, we automatically assume that training and disciplined practice are necessary to become skillful. For example, my older brother is an expert piano player, but he did not acquire his expertise by sitting down at the piano at the age of seven and deciding that he would play Chopin's *Ballade* in G minor, opus 23. He took lessons from one of the most gifted piano teachers in the U.S. While I was out playing with the football, he was inside practicing his scales and the progressively harder pieces his piano teacher challenged him with. Today he can play with skill and freedom. I cannot. The difference? Skillful teaching and disciplined application.

In the moral matters of life we naively believe things will work out by themselves, yet we do not make such an assumption for something as relatively simple as playing a musical instrument or sailing a boat. Proverbs counters this laissez-faire parental attitude by stating that wisdom's goal is to help the teenager "to internalize the art of skillful living, which comes through disciplined training; to discern the words of insight; to acquire the discipline to act with foresight and reason, doing what is right, just, and fair" (1:2-3).

What standards should we live by? How do we apply those standards in everyday situations? How do we apply those principles fairly? The answers to these difficult questions do not come by chance. They come to those who receptively listen to the instruction of wise teachers who believe in God's standards. And they come to those who discipline themselves to learn to make distinctions between choices that will result in good and those that yield disaster. The goal of Proverbs is for parents and their children to learn to internalize the ability to live a skillful life. This skill can only be gained through discipline.

The introduction to Proverbs concludes with a promise to teenagers who respond to the instruction: they will become the proud owners of a wise head on young shoulders.

The Naïve Novice

> To give shrewdness to the naive, to give to the young the ability to formulate successful life plans. (1:4)

No teenager wants to be called a naive novice! So why does God use this label to address one of the principal groups He wants to reach?

The dictionary defines *novice* as an individual who has no previous training or experience in a specific field or activity. For example, a novice in snow skiing decked out in designer skiwear seeks to accomplish the seemingly impossible feat of making it over to the beginner slope. With teaching, the beginner will learn the art of the snow plow. Add a little disciplined commitment, and the advanced techniques of the parallel and stem will not be out of reach. The novice has the potential to become an expert and to experience the exhilaration and freedom of skiing down a treacherous, advanced slope in full control.

However, if this novice is a "know-it-all" who pridefully rejects expert help, choosing rather to learn in the school of hard knocks, he will probably end up with a broken leg, a ski pole through his calf, or his feet in the air after a head-first fall into an eight-foot snow bank. Obviously, the purpose of Proverbs is not to teach skiing, but it is to teach the inexperienced beginner how to skillfully get down the treacherous slope of life like an expert.

God is not being critical when He refers to teenagers as naive novices. By definition, the young have not lived long enough to acquire the knowledge and discipline necessary to be experts in the art of living. The crucial issue is whether they will remain naive or be willing to receive instruction.

Leafing through the proverbial pages, we develop a composite snapshot of a beginning student in the school of wisdom. Gullibility, a cocky openness to all kinds of enticing persuasion, is the main characteristic of this student (14:15). Assertive independence causes such youth to believe they are experienced men and women in a world far advanced beyond the limited horizons of their parents. This naivete makes them easy prey for the get-rich-quick schemes of a con artist or a criminal (1:10; 16:29), or for the seduction of a foxy huntress (7:7-10; 9:16-17). They are especially vulnerable when the naive teenager's mom and dad buy into this illusion of sophistication and experienced judgment. With carefree abandon, this teenager clings to his open-minded life-style (1:22). Like five-inch sunfish playing with a worm, he is oblivious to the fatal steel hook at the heart of some of the juiciest, most attractive temptations.

The disciplined teaching of Proverbs can expose evil's lures. But if the naive teen stubbornly rejects this teacher or ignorantly refuses to take the time to listen, he can become hardened in his inescapable, foolish behavior (14:18). That behavior can even result in death as Proverbs 1:32 says: "For the turning away of the simple will slay them, and the complacency of fools will destroy them"

(NASB*). I used to believe that Proverbs exaggerated things slightly at this point, but after seventeen years in the pastorate I have experienced heartache at gravesites with dads and moms of teens who did not follow the life-giving principles of Proverbs.

It's not all bad news, however, for naive novices. They are still young and still open-minded. Maybe they will be open to the call of wisdom. God keeps trying to reach their number (1:22, 32). By observing the disgrace that comes to someone who chooses to laugh at wisdom's teaching, they might learn about life's realities before it is too late (22:3). This is the successful ingredient of programs such as Scared Straight in which kids experimenting with drugs are taken into prison where they can see firsthand where their life-style could lead them.

There's still time for them to learn and live. Proverbs claims it can help the naive to become worldly-wise yet remain innocent (1:4). Jesus taught us to be wise as serpents concerning the temptation of evil yet harmless as doves concerning the experience of it (Matthew 10:16). The Star Wars generation has a good chance to live wisely, unless we parents fail to give them the right stuff.

THE NAIVE PARENT

When you are young you cannot help but be somewhat naive. When you are old, however, there is no excuse. One of the things that concerns me as I counsel families is the lack of mature parents who genuinely assume the adult responsibility to train the next generation. One parent responds to the invasion of adolescence by frantically tightening down the screws of control while another prematurely removes the controls completely. Proverbs pleads with parents to open their ears, so they will become genuinely wise in their own lives. Then they can effectively motivate kids to follow their example.

*New American Standard Bible.

Let the experienced adult listen so that he can
increase his effectiveness in training the young.
Let the individual who already discerns how to make
right choices
acquire the ability to steer others in the right direction.
(1:5)

Wise parents always have ears tuned in to the wisdom channel.

Gary's parents were not naive. They listened to wisdom and built their home on the principles and values we are exploring in this book. They took the time to teach Gary how to skillfully sail in life.

Cathy's parents told her repeatedly that they loved her. They bragged about her physical beauty, and she never lacked spending money. Every Sunday they went to church together, but the dual careers of her parents made it impossible to have much family time. There was little opportunity for discussion. It's hard to think through moral values together when everyone is busy. Consequently, Cathy never internalized wisdom. During her three years of silence toward her parents, they prayed for one more chance to spend time together.

One evening their front doorbell rang, and Jason, Cathy's fifteen-year-old brother, answered the door. A frail woman stood on the threshold. Her complexion was pitted, her clothes dirty, her speech slightly slurred. He did not recognize her at first, but then Jason shouted. "Dad, Mom! It's Cathy!"

Slowly Cathy's parents gathered the pieces of her story together. Mick had baited Cathy with luxurious living. He praised her looks and assured her of his devoted worship. He had never found such meaning in a relationship with another woman, he said. He promised to empty his bank account to make her dreams come true. How could she have known that he was heavily involved in organized crime?

When Cathy had a bad "crack" trip that generated strong psychotic tendencies, he dumped her. Unlike many runaways, somehow she stumbled home alive. The school of experience was nearly fatal, but she was now ready to listen to advice. With skilled counseling perhaps she could gather together the pieces of her life.

Gary made choices quite different than Cathy's. Six years after their high school graduation he was again on the sidelines at a Friday night football game. This time he was not there to play football but to begin a career as an assistant coach and teacher.

Four years at the University of Texas studying history and physical education, followed by two years in a master's program in secondary education, led him to the teaching and coaching opportunity.

During the first year of his master's program, Gary attended a Christian singles fellowship in Austin. He did a poor job of hiding his excitement when Matt, a friend from church, introduced him to a new girl who had come down for the weekend from Dallas to visit her parents. Her brunette hair and sparkling hazel eyes caught his attention, but it was her gentle smile that continued to capture his attention throughout the evening.

"Hi, I'm Gary!"

"I know," she replied. "I'm Susan Morgan. Matt mentioned you earlier this evening as someone I should get to know."

For the next year Gary and Susan wore a groove into Interstate 35 between Austin and Dallas as their dating intensified. After Gary's graduation, on a beautiful spring evening in June, Susan, who was Cathy's former roommate, married the man who loved her. After honeymooning in the mountains of Colorado, they moved back to Gary's hometown in East Texas to begin his teaching and coaching responsibilities. They had skillfully maneuvered through the challenges of courtship and dating, but now the hard work of building a marriage began. Would they choose to continue in the school of wisdom?

Three teenagers, six years, many choices, and different results in life. Life-changing choices—we must all make them, and we never stop making them. Cathy was unprepared, so she had to learn in the school of experience. Susan and Gary took the less painful course of following the advice of skilled teachers. Each individual will continue to face the challenge of whether or not he or she will live according to right principles.

Which path will our children take? They will decide for themselves, but our parental responsibility is to introduce them to a Life Planner they can respect and trust. One of their most important decisions will be whether they find the kind and good Architect. Is life the throw of the dice on a Las Vegas game table or the discovery of a meaningful Designer?

THINK ABOUT IT

1. For a few minutes think about the fundamental values of your home. In order of priority, write down the top five. Think of some concrete life situations in which you fleshed out these values for your children by your example. What are some opportunities this week to do this?

2. Why do we as parents insist on obedience but become impatient with the "why" questions from our children? What are some situations in which an explanation cannot be given? How can answering "why?" become a valuable opportunity to coach our children in life?

3. What in-depth discussions have you had with your children concerning spiritual values? What precipitated these special times of communication? When was the last time your child talked openly about what was happening inside him or her? What led up to that discussion and caused it to occur? What could you do to encourage that more often?

4. Interview your kids with the question: What do we do when you try to open up to us that turns you off? How can we overcome this?

2

Respecting the Architect

Have you ever complained about your monthly house payment? For many young married couples today these payments are as unreasonable as buying the Taj Mahal on credit. To beat this credit crunch Mary and I decided to try the do-it-yourself approach. We enlisted the help of a friend and then went to the bank. After obtaining the loan, we went to a local lumber yard and told them we needed the raw materials to build a house. A few days later two large, tractor trailers lumbered slowly toward our newly purchased acre of land and dumped a pile of two-by-fours, two-by-sixes, nails, bricks, wire, and roofing materials. Our house just waited to be assembled. Our day of creative freedom had arrived.

Not exactly sure of what we wanted in a house, Mary and I decided the best approach would be to start mixing cement, nailing boards, gluing PVC, and stringing wire. What an adventure it would be to see what would evolve! Trial and error marked the evolution of our home, but our construction slogan remained "We do it our way." After two years of creative learning by experience, what to our wondering eyes should appear but—a total disaster!

Obviously, this account is untrue. Mary and I did build our home with the help of a friend, but it was not a haphazard, do-your-own-thing affair. The friend who volunteered to help us was an expert who had built many homes already. Even though interest rates were high, the bank would not give us any money until we presented detailed architectural blueprints of every inch of the proposed structure. Through constant use, these plans became dog-eared and soiled. Daily they guided us in the construction process. Six months after the foundation was poured, our family moved into a home of beauty and strength.

Why do we think it foolish to try to build a house without the skill of an experienced architect and builder, but the laissez-faire parent will attempt to build a family, a far more complex task, without a life Architect? In fact, many contemporary "wise men" tell us that no personal life Architect or Builder exists.

A LIFE ARCHITECT?

Astronomer and Pulitzer prize-winning author Carl Sagan begins his best-seller *Cosmos* with these words: "The cosmos is all that is or ever was or ever will be." A committed believer in evolution and man's ability to solve life's mysteries with the scientific method, Dr. Sagan capitalizes *Cosmos* in his writing but speaks of whatever "gods" that might exist in small letters. His faith is in his brilliant intellect, and the "god" of his philosophy is the material universe. According to this Cornell University astronomer, there is no divine Architect. We are not responsible to an eternal Father to whom we will have to give an account, he claims. For Sagan there is no divinely revealed blueprint for living. But can we be sure he has all the facts?

In contrast to this prideful worship of man and universe, let me introduce a far more humble, ancient wise man. He was not as quick to speak authoritatively about creation events that no scientist was on the scene to observe. Agur was a man with a strange-sounding name and penetrating things to say. He admitted his inability to answer the question, Is there a supreme holy One who established all things? Listen to his observations:

> If you ask me how to live a skillful life of lasting meaning or how to personally know the Supreme Being, I'm as stupid as an animal. There are theologians who profess to know all about the divine based on their own mental deductions. I am not one of them. Who has ever gone to the edge of the universe and returned? What man can control the wind or the formation of clouds in the sky? Who created the entire earth? What is the name that discloses the

true character of this Ultimate Being, and what is the name of His Son? Surely man can answer these questions if he is so wise. (30:2-3)

This ancient Near Eastern wise man saw clearly man's inability to answer life's most fundamental questions: Where did I come from? Why am I here? Where am I going? The universe is too immense, nature too profound, man's mind too limited, and life too short to resolve these vital ultimate question marks concerning how everything began and whether a personal creator is responsible for it all. But does Agur throw up his hands and cynically say, "These questions pose a philosophical Rubik's Cube® nobody can solve"?

In Proverbs 30:5 he confidently declares that the ultimate Being in the universe has chosen to reveal His answers to these questions in His errorless Word.

All of us must choose upon what kind of a foundation we will build our homes. Like Carl Sagan, some trust in man and the material world. This option involves betting your life on your ability to give the right answer to the riddle of the meaning of life. But I believe it is far safer to build a home upon the premise that the Bible is able to identify our Creator and provide His credentials.

THE ARCHITECT'S CREDENTIALS

I worked construction as a carpenter's helper during the summers of my first two years in seminary. If you have ever done construction work, you are well aware of the elite status on the job site that this position enjoys. All the important jobs—pulling nails out of used lumber, jack-hammering down the concrete in pier holes that have been poured eight inches too high, and running around to keep your union carpenter's nail pouch filled—belong to the "carpenter's helper," or more accurately his "go-for." No one even turned his head when I came on the job in the morning. In contrast, when my superintendent got word that the architect was coming to inspect the job, everyone began to scurry. The architect deserved respect because he designed the building, and he would judge how accurately his plans were being followed.

Proverbs 3:19-20 reveals that God deserves infinitely more respect than any architect on a construction site. Why? Because He designed and built the cosmos. His basic credential as the Creator could not be stated more clearly: "The Lord by wisdom founded the earth; by understanding He established the heavens; by His knowledge the depths were broken up, and clouds drop down the dew."

These verses identify God not only as the designing Architect but also as the Contractor who created the stars and, more important, the earth, which is our physical home. Trial and error probability factors were not His construction principles. Rather, every detail was carried out according to the brilliant blueprint in His mind. He was not only the expert who created matter and built the universe, but He also maintains His creation. Even the rain against our window pane falls according to God's design.

This design is personified for us in Proverbs. Observe how wisdom presents herself not only as God's blueprint for building the universe but also as a master craftsman who daily worked at His side.

> The Lord conceived me at the beginning of His work
>   before His deeds of old;
> I was appointed from eternity,
>   from the beginning, before the world existed.
> When there were no oceans, I was given birth,
>   when there were no springs overflowing with water;
> before the mountains were sunk into place,
>   before the hills, I was born,
> before He made the earth or its fields
>   or any of the dust of the world.
> I was there when He established the heavens,
>   when He traced out the horizon's circle on the face of
> the ocean,
>   when He established the clouds above
>   and firmly established the subterranean springs.
> I was there when He set boundaries for the sea
>   so that the water would not overflow His command
> and when He marked off the foundations of the earth.
>   Then I was at His side—a master craftsman!
> Daily I was filled with pleasure,
>   always rejoicing in His presence.

I rejoiced in every detail of His earth,
    but I was especially delighted with mankind.
                                    (8:22-31)

Have you ever wondered what happened before there was time? Verses 22-26 reveal some answers from the eternal Creator. So our childlike minds could begin to understand, He describes His creation of the cosmos like a human builder would describe a construction project. First He pictures Himself as an architect at a drafting table. "Wisdom" represents the skillful ideas and drawings that He develops for the construction of the universe.

The project begins (vv. 27-29). Wisdom now represents not only the project drawings but also a master craftsman skillfully plying her trade in the creation process (vv. 30-31). Daily the Lord and wisdom take great pleasure in their accomplishments, echoing the declaration of Genesis 1: "It is good." Did you notice what wisdom's greatest joy was? In the midst of all the natural wonders, her greatest joy was the creation of mankind (v. 31).

So why is this significant to our discussion of how to teach our kids to live right? The reason is simple: life is not like the roll of the dice on a Las Vegas game table. Just as skillfully thought-out principles guided the construction of the universe, so the wise principles for right living taught in Proverbs need to guide the construction of our lives. The principles presented are not just nice ideas that an old-fashioned religionist concocted on Saturday night to fill in the blanks for a Sunday school class. They belong to the essential nature of the created universe. No one can escape these moral realities.

Wisdom concludes her discussion of creation with a message to our teenagers.

Now then, teens, listen receptively to me.
    Those who obediently follow my lifestyle live happily.
Obey my instruction and you will be wise.
    Do not neglect me!
Happy is the individual who listens to me,
    who daily watches at my door and waits on my door-
        step
    so as not to miss a thing.

For whoever finds me finds life itself
and receives acceptance from the Lord.
But the one who misses me, hates himself.
Everyone who hates me loves death.

(8:32-36)

Wisdom promises that she can make our kids happy. If we discipline them to learn and to obey her principles, she promises to give them happy, meaningful lives. But if they reject her, it's deadly. Her point is that as certainly as the natural universe was built according to skillful design principles, so God means for us to build our lives according to His skillful, moral principles. To try to live in rebellion against His moral plan is like trying to breathe under water like a goldfish for an hour. We were not designed to breathe water. We have the freedom to try, but after twenty minutes we will be dead. You can stand at the top of the Empire State building and declare you do not believe in gravity. You can sincerely believe you can fly. But once you jump, you cannot prevent the splat on the pavement below. Likewise, if we try to live in defiance of the life-giving principles of wisdom, we will self-destruct. To reject Proverbs' blueprint for living is to reject reality! The reality is that wisdom is man's best friend. If we fail to follow this blueprint or if we hate its demands on our lives, we will only discover that we have fallen in love with disaster (vv. 32-36).

"OK!" you might say. "God's life plan needs to be obeyed because He is the original Designer. What's His daily schedule look like now? Is God an Architect who drew up the original prints for the universe and then moved on to more important heavenly projects? Is He on the scene inspecting and evaluating what I do in His creation?" According to God's credentials, He is not only creation's Architect, but He is also our Judge.

HERE COMES THE JUDGE

Unlike a human judge or father who can be faked out, God sees everything. We can never get away with something behind God's back. In fact, it is impossible to get behind His back. He sees all and knows all! Listen to these revelations:

The eyes of the Lord are in every place keeping watch on both the wicked and the good. (15:3)

Not even the mysteries of death and destruction pose any problem for God's knowledge. How much easier do you think it is for Him to know every thought in our hearts. (15:11)

We can always rationalize our actions, but God knows our innermost motivations. (16:2; 21:2)

The powerful beam of God's searchlight turns the darkest corners of our thoughts to broad daylight. (20:27)

A prostitute in Dallas came to us for counseling and asked me to ask God to take a vacation for a while. Her scheme was that while His back was turned, she could turn a $200 trick to help pay her debts and then come back and pick up with God where she left off. We pitied her failure to understand that no one can ever escape God's observation. But what about the secret things we think we get away with when nobody is looking? Few of us would so easily forget God's standards if we remembered that from God's perspective we do everything at the fifty-yard line of a heavenly stadium with all the lights blazing and God observing all the action "up close and personal."

As Judge over His creation God not only knows everything that goes on, but as supreme Ruler He supervises everything. Not even the wicked, who totally disregard their Creator, can escape from the ultimate day of reckoning with Him. In the end, He brings everything to its appropriate conclusion (16:4). Our minds devise all kinds of plans, but actually our lives are controlled by His plans (16:9; 19:21; cf. James 4:13-17). Pridefully, we deceive ourselves into believing that we can choose our own steps through life. In fact, every event in our lives comes from God, and we can never completely figure out the reasons for every happening (20:24).

Have your kids ever cunningly come up with a plan that faked you out? No one has ever come up with a scheme that could beat God (21:30). Our minds are so limited that they cannot even predict the headlines for a single day with certainty, but God knows and supervises the events of each day (27:1). Confronted with His supreme will, the only wise course is to bow before Him in trust.

But can He be trusted? Can we be sure He's not a gigantic, cosmic being playing a video game with human bleeps, coldly pushing the restart button when a human self-destructs? Yes, we can be sure! Proverbs teaches us that though He is the powerful Creator and Judge, He is also the perfect Father. His goal is to make us just like Himself.

FATHER KNOWS BEST

Proverbs 3:11-12 exposes God's caring, fatherly discipline: "My son, do not reject the Lord's discipline. Do not resent it when He corrects you, because the Lord corrects the son He loves. Like a father He corrects the son He delights in!"

Earthly dads sometimes punish kids for unfair reasons. We fail to take the time to see the situation correctly. God never messes up in His child-training. It is always for our good. He is a fatherly coach training us to reign as His heirs by His side forever. Check out Hebrews 12:5-11. Our heavenly Creator, Judge, and Father wants us to base our lives on three foundational commitments to Him: reverence, trust, and intimacy. These are the commitments we and our children need to make to Him.

FOUNDATIONAL CONSTRUCTION COMMITMENTS

We had an eighty-two-year-old great-grandmother in our church family whose questions prodded me to think carefully concerning the Word of God. One Wednesday night after Bible study she came up to me and asked, "Dave, you taught us tonight the basic motto of Proverbs—'The fear of the Lord is the beginning of knowledge but hardened fools despise skillful living which comes through discipline' (1:7). Am I to teach my great-grandchildren to be afraid of God, to shiver with fright when the roar of a tornado ravages across the Texas plains?"

Nonie nailed me with the kind of question that my doctoral level seminary jargon could not satisfy. Is God saying that great-grandmothers should tell little children scary ghost stories about Himself? Does the fear of God mean that we should shiver with fright at the mention of His name?The following illustration has helped clarify my thinking concerning what Proverbs means when it speaks about the "fear of the Lord," a subject it discusses often (1:7; 8:13; 9:10; 10:27; 14:27; 15:33; 19:23; 22:4).

Suppose one night you find yourself in Harlem, New York City, at 2:00 A.M. The tenement buildings cast menacing shadows on the deserted streets. Suddenly, a gang of leather-coated hoodlums emerges from an alley. Their switchblades snap open, and they force you to take off running for your life. Up one alley, down the other! Your lungs crave air, but the whirring of the gang's "yoyos," steel balls with spikes through them, drives you on. Quickly, you turn down a long, narrow alley. You're just thirty feet from the end when a hulk of a man steps out of the shadows and blocks your escape. He's seven feet of rippling muscles, big enough and strong enough to play defensive end on any NFL team. You freeze in your tracks. Where can you turn now? The gang blocks your entrance, and the incredible monster blocks your escape. With no place to run, you look into the eyes of the massive man blocking your path. Then his loving hand beckons you to come. Your heart beating wildly, you scurry behind the safety of his right knee. In that moment, terrified dread becomes reverential trust in your protector. The hoodlums are no match for his power, and you are safe in his care on a dark night in Harlem.

To fear the Lord is to realize that God wants to use His awesome creative power not to destroy our lives but to save and care for them. We are born into a dangerous world like Harlem. The norm is that no one gets off the planet alive. Satan, the father of lies and murder, stalks us in the alleys of life. Two thousand years ago Jesus Christ, the promised Savior, stepped out of the shadows of eternity to fight for our eternal safety. Suspended on a Roman cross, He paid our sentence for sin in full. Easter morning He left a guarded tomb empty. His resurrection demonstrated that He alone has the power to give life that can never be snuffed out. Today He blocks your path and summons you to depend upon Him to give you spiritual life that will last forever. Have you personally realized that He died for you and that His hand invites you to His protection so that awesome dread can become reverential trust in Jesus as your Protector?

The most famous verses in Proverbs are an invitation to humbly put all your confidence in the Lord.

Trust in the Lord with your entire personality. Don't depend upon your own insights to make right choices in life. In every life situation be intimate with God, and He will make your paths straight. (3:5-6)

Remember the ancient wise man's questions: "Who created the entire earth? What is the name that discloses the true character of this Ultimate Being, and what is the name of His Son?" The answer is: God is the Creator, Judge, and Father. His Son's name and the name that discloses His true character is Jesus Christ. The foundational step in becoming wise is to kneel in reverence and trust before Him. When we trust in our Heavenly Father's love as expressed in the sacrifice of His Son on Calvary, we can enjoy intimate closeness with Him.

I was seven years old when someone explained to me that Jesus paid the penalty for my sin on the cross and wanted to help me live a skillful life. I put my confidence in Him. Have you made this commitment?

God wants us to put our arms at our sides and rest quietly in His hands. He wants us to stop depending on our own insights into how to live and to stop believing that human ingenuity can solve the riddles of life and death. He wants to teach us that the real purpose for living is intimacy with Him. In fact, the intimacy He desires is so warm that the term used to describe it in Proverbs 3:6 is frequently used in the Old Testament of the sexual intimacy enjoyed by a husband and wife. This ultimate intimacy can only begin to express the oneness God wants to enjoy with us. Rather than our stumbling down a dark, garbage-filled alley, God wants to guide us down a straight path that leads to the right destination (4:18-19).

God is on the job site. We need to respect the divine Architect. If we follow the plans of the proud humanist who tells his own story about the cosmos, we will ultimately be rebuked by the God we disbelieved in. But if we depend upon His revelation, the divine Architect promises us eternal life. Reverence, trust, and intimacy—these provide the proverbial concrete foundation for living that will never crack.

Think About It

1. Discuss with your teenagers how they believe mankind arrived on earth. If someone believes that man is simply the product of matter and time and chance, how does that influence his views toward the uniqueness of the human personality, human love, and moral standards? Read Matthew 19:4-6. Did Jesus believe that the creation account of Genesis was a fairy tale? Who does He say created human beings? Why would the viewpoint of Jesus Christ be more dependable than Carl Sagan's?

2. Jot down some characteristics of God's personality you have learned from this chapter. Children tend to think of God as being like their parents; what are some characteristics of your personality that accurately reflect traits in God's personality? What deviations need to be dealt with?

3. Have you personally explained to your children who Jesus is, how He died for their sins, and how He rose from the dead and is alive today? It is important that they relate to Him as a person and make their own decision concerning their beliefs about Him. Your beliefs will not insure their standing before the divine Architect.

3

The Demolition Crew

There is an Architect. More impressive, He's a loving, personal Father. Our parental responsibility is to work with Him as His Spirit seeks to woo our children to a relationship of reverence, trust, and intimacy with Himself. Proverbs sketches His blueprint for a skillfully constructed life. Our children are born in naivete about this life plan, gullible to believe all kinds of false information, vulnerable to evil's seduction. Our prayers can help them to open their ears to wisdom's voice.

In chapter 2 we met Lady Wisdom, the master craftsman over all creation. She personifies not only the facts of nature but also the facts of life—moral norms intrinsic to God's created order. Wisdom loves mankind. Human beings, the masterpiece of God's creative genius, are her pride and joy.

As we turn to Proverbs 2, we find Lady Wisdom out on the streets of our contemporary lives, no longer in the idyllic surroundings of Eden. She is a street preacher, aggressively calling to our children, warning against the peril of rejecting her call. How can our kids hear her voice? How can they be protected from joining the deadly laughter of the scoffer, the complacency of the moral dullard, or the hardness of the impenetrable block—three demolition experts intent on swinging a wrecking ball against their young lives? We need to make our public and private message consistent if we want our kids to heed her voice.

WISDOM'S PUBLIC ADDRESS

Wisdom preaches enthusiastically in the street;
   she raises her voice in the public squares;
   she proclaims at the head of the bustling thoroughfares;
   she presents her message in the large gathering areas
      by the city gates.

(1:20-21)

The proverbial principles need to be heard in the privacy of our homes. But our kids must also see that our values are worth standing up for in public, in the teeth of ridicule. The wisdom teachers of ancient Israel never contented themselves with merely communicating their insights privately to their own families. They aggressively interacted in the marketplace, the city halls, and the educational centers of their society. Instead of bolting up their insights behind safe monastery walls, they declared them in the public arena.

The ultimate wisdom teacher reflected this strategy of taking the message to the people. Jesus' voice could be heard in the synagogue, the religious environment of His day, but He also sat down to teach in homes, by a lake, and on the hillsides. He walked among fisherman, tax-collectors, prostitutes, housewives, and soldiers, zealously challenging them to submit to the wisdom and authority of His Father. Our kids need to see us mimicking His method as we take the Father's message into our Monday morning world. The parents in Proverbs were not intimidated by the criticism, "Spiritual values are an individual, private affair. They should not be soiled in the public debates of the marketplace."

As a young boy, traveling with my dad into New York City to the radio stations was special. He loved live talk shows where his personal commitment to Jesus Christ would be publicly challenged. With my hand clasped tightly in his, we maneuvered through the crowded streets. Proudly I carried, sometimes dragged, his heavy, tan briefcase. I remember walking through the revolving door of a major network one evening. No cordial greeting or handshake welcomed us. Ten seconds before air time the host simply nodded through his cigarette smoke toward the red "On the Air" light. The engineer's hand gave the signal and the program began. "Jack

Wyrtzen, what's so special about J. C.? You have the audacity to go around this country trying to compel people to believe in Jesus Christ for their eternal destiny. Who does J. C. think He is?"

Dad did not shrink before the ridicule. Like the apostle Paul in Acts he responded to pressure with his testimony. "For eighteen years I treated the name of Jesus lightly, just as you do. 'Jesus Christ' was an expletive to be shouted when life got exasperating. Then during a week of Army Reserve training a buddy began to explain to me the Carpenter's true identity and the gift of forgiveness He wrapped up for me on the cross. One night through reading the Scriptures I finally understood—Jesus was the Son of God. He loved me enough to cancel my unpayable debt of sin."

I heard Dad proclaim the gospel to agnostic radio hosts, atheists, and so-called sex experts. He preached not only to crowds in Madison Square Garden but also to the attendants taking quarters on the Garden State Parkway. Many of those attendants knew him by name and had to ask for a different tract than the one he was now offering a second time.

My dad, who prayed with my brother and me before turning the light out in our bedroom at the close of a day, was not ashamed to proclaim his faith on the city streets. This combination of private integrity and public courage strongly shaped my personal commitment to the wisdom of God. I must pass this heritage of public testimony on to my children. You must pass it on to yours.

What kind of response should we expect when we go public for wisdom in the marketplace? In Proverbs, wisdom faces three demolition experts—the scoffer, the moral dullard, and the impenetrable block. They laugh at her appeal. These three fools, so dumb they mock the Architect's blueprint, seek to swing a wrecking ball against our vulnerable children. Before our kids meet them in a university classroom, sales office, or prison, we need to hand them a personal profile of these three destroyers.

THE SCOFFER

How long will you naive ones love your naivete, and scoffers be turned on by your scoffing, and moral dullards detest knowledge? (1:22)

Kyle is a freshman at the state university. It's the first day of class, and his schedule card reads "Introduction to Religion" for fourth period. Already he feels buried under term papers, reading assignments, and lab hours from his previous classes. A class in religion looked like an excellent way to get in an interesting elective in the humanities. The bell brings his 135 fellow classmates to silence, and Dr. Carson, ivy league Ph.D. with the preppie look to match, begins his introduction.

"Students, I welcome you to class 101. My responsibility is to give you an education, specifically in the field of religion. Religion—it's the history of humanity's greatest insights but also of some of man's most opinionated stupidities. Canonical authority, the belief that the supreme Being has spoken clearly in one religious tradition or sacred writing, is one of these brainless absurdities. Did anyone happen to bring the 'Holy Bible' with him to class?"

Sally, an eighteen-year-old from a rural Southern community, digs into her purse and hands a pocket New Testament to the professor.

"Thousands of Americans have taken this book to be the breath of God. They affirm God speaks to them in its pages. Before this semester is over, I trust that no one will continue to defend this Sunday school naivete."

With a dramatic flourish he throws the Bible back to Sally and scoffs, "Holy Bible! It's no different from any other great literary classic!"

Many professors would be horrified at this radical display of nonobjectivity. Though the majority of them might not accept that God authored every word of Scripture, those who are genuinely well read in the field would know of powerful, credible defenses of the inspiration of the Bible. As a college freshmen, Kyle might not yet have access to these theological sources that would put Dr. Carson's outburst into perspective. He will probably never discover that his professor was raised in traditional Christianity and that much of his hostility reflects a continued adolescent rebellion against his parents. Kyle may be ignorant of the academic defenses of inspiration or the psychological struggles his professor has against his upbringing. He should know, however, the telltale signs of the mocker, for

Proverbs strongly warns against this spirit of arrogant "free thinking."

I remember that in my teens a finely tuned skill to mock others and be sarcastic won loud applause from the peer group. Most of us remember this loud, defiant struggle to understand ourselves. But a belly laugh in response to a cunning association of ideas in a Far Side cartoon is one thing. Laughing at God's advice in the Bible is quite another.

The naive youth who begins to pal around with the group that mocks sacred values begins a precarious slide toward disaster. Proverbs X-rays the personality of Dr. Carson the scoffer. Skillful parents hand their kids a dossier on this wise guy before sending them out into the world.

"Insolent! Arrogant! His name is 'the Scoffer'! He behaves with excessive self-conceit" (21:24).

Prideful self-sufficiency is at the scoffer's core. Defiant cynicism makes a joke of parents who give guidelines to kids (13:1). His rejection of parental authority leads to a belligerent mocking of school officials, the police, and eventually all forms of legitimate authority (15:12). Scoffers march for anarchy. Their placards call for the overthrow of all order and structure in society (29:8). Whether it is the bloodthirsty mob of Robespierre or the bombs of Libyan terrorists, scoffers are expert demolition artists but impotent builders of a peaceful, orderly society. They never question whether they can build a better replacement for the structures they blow up. Their cries of ridicule deafen their internal ability to listen to wisdom's voice (14:6).

This disdain for spiritual, parental, and governmental authority should never be honored with million-dollar contracts or classed as comedy par excellence. The scoffer should not be honored as the clever professor whose intellectualism places him beyond the influence of traditional morality. Instead, the mocking spirit should be publicly disgraced. Perhaps an open punishment will warn potential mockers against this self-destructive life-style (19:25; 21:11). Scoffer gathers around himself an admiring gang for a time, but rejection comes in the end (24:9). He cannot sustain unity. His cunning mouth instigates constant bickering and fistfights. Only exile from society will supplant his subversive plots and bring peace

(22:10; 29:8). The Creator always has the last laugh (3:34; 1:26). When you mock the Designer you end up suffering the cost alone (9:12).

There is hope, however, for this sarcastic master of double-entendre. Wisdom calls out loudly to him. The expenditure of so much energy in making a joke out of wisdom is a telltale sign—down deep inside he still cares about spiritual values. No one invests so much in resisting something that has lost all pull on his life.

But the scoffer must open his ears. Wisdom will not call forever. Tragically, the majority of this class of fools will respond to verbal correction with hatred, insult, and abuse (9:7-8; cf. Matthew 7:6). Sometimes the school of hard knocks softens their obstinacy. More often, they harden and never seek wise counsel (15:12). Their parents, like the father of the prodigal son, must allow them to leave so they may face the full force of their incorrigibility. A few look up from the pig slop and remember Daddy's fairness and love.

The second member of the demolition crew, the moral dullard, has even less time left to respond to wisdom, for he has slipped farther down toward the abyss of a ruined life. Proverbs says a great deal about this fool.

THE MORAL DULLARD

Moral dullards hate knowledge. (1:22*b*)

He who trusts in himself is a fool. (28:26*a*)

The fool is rash and self-assured. (14:16)

Their complacency will destroy them. (1:32*b*)

Here is the brutish materialist who complacently lives life for himself, with no regard for moral values. He is hardly dull intellectually, but his opinionated, incorrigible nature causes his brain cells to refuse to fire when it comes to the application of ethics in daily life. He is loud and flamboyant. His smug self-confidence could attract our sons and daughters if they meet him in the business world. They need to discern that he is living in the eye of a hurricane. Since his companions share the pain of his destructive life-style when the storms of life blow (1:27; 13:20; 28:26), our children need to be trained to see past his veneer at their first exposure.

HIS PLASTIC COATING

First impressions of Mr. Dullard are deceiving. The feistiness of the scoffer is absent in him. This fool is self-assured (1:22), quick with his tongue (12:23; 29:20), and sometimes flaunts luxurious wealth (19:10). He is able to bring loud laughter with his coarse jokes at the bar after work (10:23). When he is prosperous and his illegalities are camouflaged, society often grants him honors (26:8). But his high-flying balloon is filled with explosive hot air. Most of the time this Archie Bunker prototype rolls through life like an untended canister of nitroglycerin. He is dangerous! (17:12). His life is full but empty.

HIS HOLLOW CORE

Deception and self-deception—they are his life. Unlike the wise man who loves God's blueprint for living, the dullard detests His life plan (1:22). Rather than trusting in the Lord with all of his heart, a major foundational "spec" for building a wise life (3:6), he depends upon his inconsiderate, defiant impulses (28:26).

In school, trivia rivets his attention (17:24), whereas his ears are deaf to words that humanize life with beauty, grace, and truth (14:33; 15:7; 23:9). He views the cost of tuition at the University of Wisdom as a bad investment. His heart lacks the motivation to learn right standards (14:33; 15:7; 17:16).

The inexperienced instructor will be sucked into a mire of senseless interaction if he tries to deal with the dullard on his own terms (26:4). The experienced teacher will know when to ignore him and when the situation demands a forceful exposure of his prideful myopia (26:5).

Sometimes it appears that he has grasped an important life principle. But though he might memorize the words of a proverb, it remains as useless to him as the impotent legs of a cripple because he lacks the discretion to know how and when to apply the principle (26:7, 9). Like a horse or mule he understands the language of the whip but cannot be controlled by words of reason (26:3).

When he goes out into the business world, dishonesty is his technique for climbing to the top (14:8; 19:1). He wounds anyone who hires him (26:10). He cheats anyone who buys from him. His heavy thumb on the scale escalates the cost of his produce (11:1; 20:23). He misrepresents those who count on him in delicate negotiations and sells out his clients to attain his own selfish ends (26:6).

If he succeeds, he might be given positions of honor and respect (26:1, 8), but eventually his shallowness will be exposed to all (13:16). His frivolous use of wealth will make him look ridiculous and coarse. He does not develop the maturity and character that enable an individual to use material things graciously for the benefit of others (19:10). Money slides through his fingers. He consumes but does not save (21:20).

In the law courts he victimizes the innocent. On the witness stand perjury means nothing to him (12:17; 14:25). Like the scoundrels who executed Jezebel's wicked plot against Naboth and put the possession of a vineyard above the value of a man's life (1 Kings 21), this fool's mind is filled with strategies to destroy others (12:20). Doing evil is his entertainment (10:23; 13:19).

Friendly words mask his evil intent, for hatred lurks in his soul (26:23-26). Since he feeds on mental junk food (15:14), his mouth gushes foolishness (15:2, 7). He never knows when to keep quiet (12:23; 13:16), speaks hastily without thinking (29:9), and explodes in anger, igniting conflict (14:16; 18:6-7; 29:11).

Seven character traits—pride, deceit, cruelty, malicious cunning, impetuous recklessness, perjury, and contentiousness—summarize his core. These are the abominable seven that turn God's stomach (6:16-19). This individual can count on an inheritance from the Lord—shame (3:35).

The child who grows to become this fool will despise his mother (15:20) and exasperate his father (10:1; 17:21, 25; 19:13). He ruins his parents (19:13). Before this becomes our own fate and before our naive kids begin to slide toward this pain and destruction, we must warn them. Anyone who associates with this kind of individual will come to ruin (13:20; 14:7). He is as dangerous as a she-bear robbed of her cubs (17:12).

As for the dullard, there is still hope for this fool. Wisdom still offers her invitation (1:22; 8:5). Sometimes, when their foolishness yields disgrace and punishment, dullards humble themselves and become receptive to wisdom's voice (26:12). The spiritual conversion of some prominent conspirators in the Watergate affair demonstrates this hope for the arrogant secularist. Like scoffers, however, most dullards continue their slide downward (14:24).

THE IMPENETRABLE BLOCK

This fool develops when scoffer's arrogance and dullard's moral complacency harden into impenetrable foolishness. He is completely convinced that he is right and everyone else is wrong (12:15; contrast 3:7). He never listens (18:13). His mouth explodes in anger at the slightest provocation (10:14; 12:16; 20:3). His outbursts constantly burden others (27:3) and continue into the courtroom as he rants and raves against his opponents in frequent lawsuits (29:9). Actually, everyone sees through his pompous charade. He's only a lightweight in the halls of government (24:7).

The blockhead is not retarded. He is capable of intense mental activity but uses his mind to plot evil instead (24:8-9). This deviousness destroys his own home (11:29; 14:1) and brings him under the discipline of the state (16:22). Though calamitous circumstances pound him like a pestle grinding crystals in a mortar, he will not turn away from his criminal activities, for foolishness has become his essence (27:22).

He curses God for his bad fate (19:3). He mocks the ideas of repentance and confession of sin (14:9). He detests the mottos of Proverbs, such as the statement that a reverential relationship with God is the beginning of a skillful life (1:7). He abhors God's wisdom and instruction. Often he goes to a premature grave still cursing his Creator (10:8, 10, 21).

While our children are still young and before they begin to slide toward mockery, moral dullness, and impenetrable hardness, we need to give them the facts concerning the outcome of these life pathways. Most of this training needs to be done before they hit the storms of adolescence. When our children exhibit the incorrigible, rebellious character traits of fools and refuse to listen to our verbal instruction, corporal discipline is required (13:24; 22:15; 23:13-14; 29:15).

This "rod of correction," however, must never be placed in the hands of rash anger. When this occurs, the parent himself becomes the deadly, dangerous fool. Proverbs should never be used to justify child abuse. Only the mature parent who knows that a positive word of instruction accomplishes far more than harsh put-downs will have the discernment to know when sarcastic mockery of parental authority or complacent indifference to right and wrong demand a spanking given in love. Only the wise parent can detect the lie in the modern naive notion that a child left to himself will turn out OK. The seed of impenetrability lies in the fertile soil of everyone's heart, including our children's, and we must challenge them to invite wisdom in before their spirits harden into concrete (14:18).

WISDOM'S PROMISE

> If only you would have turned in response to my correction, I would have poured out my spirit on you; I would have made my words known to you. (1:23)

The destiny of our kids depends upon the response of their hearts to this call of wisdom. She asks no one to clean up his internal house before she will come and take up residence in his personality. She simply asks us to stop denying our foolishness and recognize that we are heading down the wrong road. When we turn to her and humbly respond, we receive the gift of a new inner capacity to understand and apply God's design for living. The spirit of wisdom pours herself into our souls.

The New Testament presents a similar invitation. Jesus came to earth on a rescue mission. In every detail He lived His Father's blueprint for skillful living. Like Lady Wisdom He went out into the marketplace and delivered his invitation: "If anyone thirsts, let him come to me and drink. The one who believes in me, just as the Scripture has said, out of his innermost being will flow rivers of living water." The apostle John goes on to explain what Jesus was referring to. "By this He spoke concerning the Spirit, whom those who believed in Him would receive" (John 7:38-39).

Since the Day of Pentecost, the third Person of the Trinity has gone out into the world to draw children into God's family. When they believe in Jesus Christ, they receive more than simply wise counsel about life. God Himself takes up residence in their personalities to guide them into all truth (John 16:13). My greatest concern as a dad is for each of our children to open his or her life to Jesus and to put complete confidence for eternal life in Him. This moment of belief causes them to receive the Holy Spirit, who alone can enable them to fulfill God's blueprint for their lives. In Old Testament times a failure to heed the voice of wisdom could lead to premature death. Today the failure to heed the Spirit's voice as He calls us to the Savior will lead to the forfeiture of eternal life in God's presence (John 3:36).

As Mary and I have sought to make Jesus Christ the center of our home life, we have seen the Holy Spirit touch our children, convicting them of their sin and their need to accept Christ's gift of forgiveness. As parents we must be sensitive to these special moments when the Spirit desires to work.

One night all Mary wanted to do after a hectic day was to remain in a horizontal position, nestled in the soft, living room recliner. Our older boys were already deeply engrossed in an exciting video. Jenae, our youngest, was awake but in bed, and Joshua reluctantly walked toward his room.

"Mommy, we haven't read our Bible story yet!" Joshua prodded.

Another delay tactic. It's already late and a school night. Why not let it go this one night? Mary's thought pattern defended her need to stay in the relaxed position. But Josh persisted.

Wearily, Mary got up, went to Josh's room, and sat down between Josh and Jenae, who had gotten out of bed, of course, when she learned her brother would have a story. They found the place in their Bible storybook and began to read. Jenae interrupted, "Mommy, what is heaven like?"

Mary's answer led to a discussion concerning how someone could know he or she was going to heaven. This bedtime moment became the time when Jenae accepted Christ's gift of forgiveness.

Our greatest joy as parents is to know that all four of our kids have made this decision. It does not insure they will always make wise choices. It does guarantee that they possess an eternal relationship with God and have made the initial step on the path toward wisdom.

All of our children, however, must be warned concerning the consequences of ignoring the quiet voice of the Spirit's instruction. The consequences of rejecting the instructions that Dad and Mom are teaching from the Scriptures can bring a harvest of despair and premature death. In life there can come a moment when it is too late to live wisely.

WISDOM'S LAST LAUGH

But since when I called, you rejected,
> when I stretched out my hand, no one paid attention,
since you neglected all my counsel,
> and would not yield to my rebuke,
I, in turn, will laugh at your distress;
> I will do the mocking when your horror comes,
when it overwhelms you like a deadly storm,
> when distress hits like a tornado,
when pressure and tightening straits overwhelm you.
> (1:24-27)

God allows fools to insult Him and mock His instructions. His name is cursed, and His Word becomes a comedy routine. We all know men and women who flagrantly break God's principles and appear to be living the life of ease and comfort. The invitation to make wise decisions, however, is not open forever.

As we trace the character development of the fools in Proverbs from naivete to mockery to complacency, there comes a point when foolishness becomes incurable. Proverbs cries out that God will have the last laugh. This is not the cruel laugh of a vindictive, maligned master who heartlessly seeks to get even. He laughs at the tragic comedy, the pitiful absurdity of those who think they can rebel against their Creator (cf. Psalm 2:4). Like those who gorge themselves with green apples, the ones who reject God's counsel will vomit from their own stupidity (1:31). God cannot be mocked forever. We reap what we sow (Galatians 6:7). Proverbs does not teach "no fault, no consequence" living. Loving parents tell their kids the truth.

Guard against the infiltration of a fool's character traits. Bad choices can lead to irremediable consequences. Yet only God, we must remember, decides when the moral dullard becomes the impenetrable block. I am thankful that regarding eternal destiny, our Creator abounds in grace.

Three more days and this rough draft of my dissertation has to be on the registrar's desk. I was just settling down to the frustration of distilling three years of research on the prophet Hosea into something that would express the concepts God had been teaching me when the telephone rang.

"Hi! Haven't been in touch for a while. I have a friend with me who needs to talk with you. Can we come over?" The voice in the receiver belonged to Charisse, a girl in Dallas with whom our church family had been working for the past three years. We had invested hours sharing biblical principles with her and seeking to meet her needs. Yet her life continued to be a spiritual roller coaster of prostitution and drugs, apparent repentance, growth in Christ —but then the return to her cesspool. As I waited for the two girls to arrive, I complained to the Lord about bringing another person like this into our lives, especially with my rough draft unfinished on the desk. The Spirit's voice reprimanded me: "Dave, I alone decide when someone is impenetrable. I care a lot more about people than I do about academic papers."

The girls arrived, sat down in the study, and lit up cigarettes. The new girl was frail and tired. She introduced herself as Gayle, and with encouragement from her friend she launched into her story. It was tragically familiar.

Rebelling against her parents, she started taking drugs as a teenager. Light drugs led to heavier ones until she had a desperate need for a daily fix of heroin. Heroin was expensive, and her beautiful teenage body could bring a good price on the streets of Dallas, so Gayle became a prostitute. Scoring and fixing became her way of life until a dirty hypodermic needle caused her to contract an infection that severely damaged the aortic valve of her heart.

After surgery, the doctors warned her. Another infection would be deadly. But Gayle returned to her peer group and her immorality, and her abuse of her body continued. When Gayle's enslavement to drugs had destroyed her reliability as a mother, her older sister was forced to take custody of Gayle's daughter. Concluding her story, her eyes welled up with tears as she showed me the wallet-sized pictures of her little girl. She slumped in her chair and sighed. "I guess I'm hopeless."

The Bible on my desk was opened to Hosea 2. I had been working on verses 2-23 where God uses the symbol of a wife who became a prostitute to represent the character and actions of His people who had enslaved themselves to idolatry and sexual immorality. Gayle was amazed—God had firsthand experience with her kind of problem.

We talked about how God punished His unfaithful wife, first by removing her material prosperity (v. 9), then by stopping her joyous celebrations (v. 11), and finally by taking her into captivity in Assyria (11:5). Gayle began to identify. The punishment for her sin was an empty purse, hollow laughter, and enslavement to a lethal habit. Her hopeless eyes made me appreciate that Hosea 2 did not end with God the Judge forever rejecting His prostitute wife.

Gayle and I read on. We listened to God tenderly speaking to His estranged wife and proposing a new intimacy with her (vv. 14, 19-20). Israel deserved to be destroyed in consequence of her lifestyle. However, God graciously chose to love her freely and forgave her sin. Gayle and I went on to the New Testament to learn how God could justify such merciful forgiveness. He sent His Son into the world to take on not only Israel's death sentence but the sentence standing against all of us.

Like Israel, Gayle could receive forgiveness and enter into an intimate relationship with God. Because Jesus rose from the dead to live forever, He could come into her life and set her free. He could give her the power to live a new life.

God courted Gayle's heart that morning. Through the simplicity of John 3:16, He asked her to admit that she was perishing and to place all her confidence in His Son. She bowed her head, confessed her rebellion, and thanked Jesus for forgiving her. At that moment a former prostitute became the bride of Christ.

Before Gayle left the study, I contacted a woman in our church who had an effective discipling ministry with girls like Gayle, and they set up a time to get together.

Gayle did not keep the appointment. My heart sank. Was she the "fool" who blurts out a sinner's prayer and uses believers when things get too hot? A call from her mother gave me the answer. Gayle missed the discipleship appointment because she was back in the hospital.

Her continued use of heroin after her first surgery had caused Gayle to contract the same infection that had previously damaged her heart so severely. When I visited Gayle in the hospital, the prognosis wasn't good. Surgery was out of the question. She needed blood. Together we prayed that God would meet her serious physical needs, and we thanked Him that though her physical body was diseased, Christ had given her a healthy, new spiritual life. She wanted so much to be given the opportunity to live wisely for Jesus.

The following Sunday was Easter, and after a day of celebrating the resurrection, Mary and I were relaxing with our kids when the telephone rang. God had worked a miracle different from the one we had expected. Gayle was home with her Bridegroom, never to face pain again. Her mom was calling to ask if I would conduct Gayle's funeral service.

Driving to a North Dallas church for the funeral, I asked the Lord for wisdom. "Give me the sensitivity to comfort Gayle's family. Give me the courage to speak the truth in love."

Many of Gayle's street friends joined her family at the service to remember her and comfort each other. What was I to say?

Since her early teens, Gayle's life-style had hardly qualified her as an exemplary Sunday school girl. She had rejected wise counsel and mocked her parents. She had run fast and hard. The natural result of her choices was physical death at the age of twenty-five.

The text God impressed on my mind was Romans 6:23. "The wages of sin is death." I pled with Gayle's friends to recognize the twistedness of their path. Gayle's coffin silently testified that "the waywardness of the naive will slay them, the careless ease of the moral dullard will kill them" (1:32).

There comes a time in this physical life when it is too late to live wisely. But does it have to be too late to meet God?

The concluding phrase of Romans 6:23 brought a beam of sunlight to the darkness of that funeral: "But the gift of God is eternal life through Jesus Christ our Lord." I related to the mourners how Gayle had become God's daughter, His Son's bride. She was now rejoicing in Christ's presence, forever free from the consequences of her sin. The blood that Gayle's friends had given in the hospital blood bank was not able to sustain Gayle's life. But the blood Jesus gave transformed a prostitute into a virgin bride, free to live in her Husband's home forever.

4
Following the Instructions

From building a spaceship with Legos® to hooking up a new VCR, I love to follow the trial-and-error technique of assembly. While I sit cross-legged on the floor of our living room in the midst of a chaos of hundreds of tiny pieces, Mary inevitably enters and utters her stock, wifely question: "Why don't you read the instructions?"

Of course, as every husband knows, our wives are right. This business of following instructions not only keeps us from shocking ourselves on the back of our TV or breaking a vital piece on our son's Lego Launcher; it can also protect us and our children from being smashed by the demolition crew we met in chapter 3. The University of Wisdom stresses the importance of following directions. The requirements for admission into this life-transforming educational program are "three Rs": receptive ears, retentive minds, and a requesting mouth. Wise parents learn how to grab their kids' attention.

RECEPTIVE EARS

Tuning your ears to wisdom. (2:2a)

Listen, children, to your father's instruction. (4:1a)

My son, pay attention to my wisdom, open your ears to my discernment. (5:1)

When Mom has told the kids, "Time for supper!" three times and has been ignored every time, she goes again to the back door and screams, "Now listen to me! Supper is on the table."

When a preacher becomes intense and wants to wake up his audience for his big idea he shouts, "Listen to me, people! Listen to me!"

Jesus himself used a favorite expression, "He who has ears to hear, let him hear." Any teacher knows that was not empty tautology. The presence of a built-in receiver on both sides of our head does not guarantee our reception of the message. Listening with the mind in gear has become a rare commodity among students. This is tragic, for an open ear is the first fundamental in the learning process. I still remember one of my coaches in the ninth grade. He began with the basics and taught us not only how to win in football but also how to excel in academics. "When your seat warms the chair in class," he would growl, "turn up the volume in your ears. It pays to listen. Your necessary study time will be cut in half if you learn to pay attention." Though everyone agreed his advice made sense, few obeyed.

Throughout four years of college and nine years of graduate school, I observed many students sleeping through lectures all day, then studying all night to learn what they had not learned while they slept in class. The wise student learns that it pays to be alert during lectures. The wise parent challenges his children from an early age to learn the discipline of attentiveness. Listen! It is the first fundamental in the school of wisdom.

RETENTIVE MIND

And hide away my commandments as a treasure deep within. (2:2a)

My son, do not forget my teaching, but guard my commandments in your heart. (3:1)

Let loyalty and dependability never leave you; bind them around your neck, inscribe them upon the tablet of your heart. (3:3)

Grasp a father's instruction firmly, do not let it slip away; guard it securely, for it is your life. (4:13)

The computer threatens to make memorization obsolete in the modern home and classroom. Who needs to remember basic facts when you can have millions of bytes of information available at the push of the "enter" key? The "new curriculum" movement in public education discouraged "rote" learning and instead stressed the importance of allowing the child to develop on his own. "Create an environment where they can discover their own truth."

The ancient Israelites rejected this naivete. A child left to himself without guidance would discover not truth but foolishness. They believed it unfair to ask every generation to rediscover the wheel in morals. Consequently, the older generation passed on to the younger generation the basics of a meaningful, godly life. Children were expected to memorize these fundamentals.

What appears to the English reader to be a haphazard collection of proverbs with little connection between them is to the Hebrew reader a series of memory devices. The repetition of key words, the use of similar sounds, and the use of an acrostic poem (each verse of Proverbs 31:10-31 begins with a successive letter of the Hebrew alphabet) help the information to stick in the student's mind. You can almost hear the Israelite parents in Proverbs exhorting their kids to memorize their Bible verses—"Hide away my commandments!" "Don't forget what I taught you!" "Inscribe these dependable principles not just on your clay tablets but on the flesh of your heart." The godly parents warned their children, "Don't let wisdom slip through your fingers."

Some modern educators are returning to this wise method of learning. Children do need to control a basic body of facts early in their education if they are going to be able to communicate with their culture. In his book *Cultural Literacy: What Every American Needs to Know,* E. D. Hirsch of the University of Virginia argues that a distaste for memorization denies a child's basic fascination with committing information to memory as indicated by spontaneous memorization of sports trivia and the complex rules of football, baseball, and basketball. When education ignores the necessity of memorization at an early age, it denies the child access to the common store of information available to educated individuals at the critical period when he has the greatest ability to retain information. Hirsch concludes, "To thrive, a child needs to learn the traditions of the particular human society and culture it is born into. Like children everywhere, American children need traditional information at a very early age."*

Proverbs agrees with Dr. Hirsch about the importance of memorizing traditions. But the traditions in Proverbs are far more important than the shared values of a human society. The Creator of all societies has put His stamp of approval upon the curriculum of wisdom presented in Proverbs.

As a child I had the ability to commit large portions of Scripture to memory quickly. Sometimes Dad would motivate me to learn Scripture by giving me a challenge: "I'll give you five dollars for every psalm you memorize." He eventually had to lower his price, so I wouldn't break his bank account. At summer camp, points were given for every verse we repeated to our counselor. If our team was behind, I would quickly learn a series of verses with the rest of my cabin in an attempt to make up the difference in points for our team. I am thankful for this stress upon the memorization of Scripture in my youth. Some of this mechanical repetition of words stuck with me. Tragically, much was soon lost. We need to begin to explain to our children the meaning of Scripture and not be content to have them simply repeat words.

Mechanical, word-perfect repetition of phrases is not the goal of the wise teacher. Students of Proverbs fail if they can only repeat phrases. They must also learn to "treasure" the principles because they have become full of meaning in their souls (2:2). Memorization with understanding shapes attitudes. Attitudes in turn become the basis of right action in the future. But what do you do when you can't figure out what a proverb is saying, when it sits limply in your mind devoid of meaning? This brings us to the third of the three Rs in the school of wisdom.

THE REQUESTING MOUTH

> And if you urgently call out to discernment, if you raise
> your voice for understanding, if you seek her as if you
> were hunting for silver ore, just like you would hunt for
> buried treasure, then you will understand. (2:3-4)

*E. D. Hirsch, Jr., *Cultural Literacy* (Boston: Houghton Mifflin, 1987), p. 31.

If any of you lacks wisdom, he should ask God and it will
be given to him, for God is a generous giver who neither
grudges or reproaches anyone. (James 1:5, RSV*)

What do we do when the text of Proverbs becomes only a se-
quence of words on the page? How should we respond when the
material doesn't make sense? When our Bible reading grows cold,
Proverbs encourages us to cry out to the Author.

Although I have a doctorate degree in biblical studies and am a
pastor, which requires studying the Bible, there are times when my
insight into Scripture is empty and my motivation to keep digging
disappears. During such silence the temptation is to rationalize:
"Isn't it hypocrisy to keep reading when you don't feel like it, when
you see no significance in these words?" An honest talk with the
Author is the only antidote for these devotion-time blues. I confess
the resistance of my heart. Instead of allowing guilt about my feelings to cause me to turn away from God, I turn toward Him in
prayer. By talking directly to Him I reaffirm my objective belief in
His presence, in spite of my subjective feeling that He is absent. I
cry out to Him to clarify what He is saying about Himself, about
me, about life. After praying, I continue to maintain the discipline
of consistent reading. His treasure and insight into the realities of
life is only for those who are willing to dig deep.

From bike riding to mastering a word processor, every learning process involves times of apparent regression when you feel like
you are getting nowhere. Why not quit? Because quitters never experience the thrill of uncovering the gold.

Proverbs compares the motivation required to become skillful
in life to the diligence of the fever-pitched treasure hunter who sells
everything he has and pours his life into finding the buried treasure
(2:4; 4:7). But wisdom pays even higher dividends than doubloons
buried in the hull of a wrecked Spanish galleon at the bottom of the
Caribbean. We must cry out to God to give us and our children an
intense hunger for the riches in His Word.

A few summers ago I had the privilege of speaking at a career
conference for young people in Poland. Though the Communist

Revised Standard Version.

government was still in power, we were allowed to teach the Scriptures freely and to interact with the young adults. Those believers had never had the opportunity to choose what style of Christian music they listened to on the radio or whether they preferred Swindoll, MacArthur, or Stanley for their daily Bible lesson. There were no arguments over which translation was closer to the original. They cherished any translation. They coveted any moments God gave them to freely discuss the Bible.

One evening after I had lectured on Proverbs for more than an hour, the young people began to fire questions at me through the translator. Their questions continued until about 1:00 A.M. I'll never forget the words of one of the Polish students when he saw me beginning to tire. "I know you're still recovering from jet lag and you have taught us many hours, but we don't often have this opportunity to sit down with a pastor and ask him our questions about the Bible. May I ask just one more?"

In spite of the difficulties of listening to me through a translator, these students were diligently hunting for the truth. As I went up to my room that night I prayed, "Lord, you have given me the privilege to live in a land of religious freedom. You allowed me to attend Dallas Theological Seminary where I was able to spend hours finely tuning the tools of Greek and Hebrew and theological discipline. All that training equipped me to study your Word and to expose it to others. But do I have the intense desire to know You and Your truth that these students have shown tonight?"

If we are to become wise with our children, our entire being— our ears, our mind, and our mouth—must get involved in this search for wisdom. As parents we are responsible for implementing the three Rs in our own lives. We cannot force our children to follow these instructions, but we can whet their appetites by showing them the benefits we have received from following God's instructions. We can remind them of the rich rewards this pursuit will bring into their lives. Wisdom is well worth the effort.

THE REWARDS OF FOLLOWING THE DIRECTIONS

Then you will understand the fear of the Lord,
   you will find intimate relationship with God. . . .

Then you will discern God's standards,
   how to apply these standards in real life situations,
   and how to do this with grace and fairness. . . .
Discretion will keep watch over you,
   understanding will guard you,
to deliver you from the way of evil,
   from men whose words are perverted. . . .
To deliver you from the immoral woman,
   from the adulteress with her smooth words. . . .
So that you might walk in the way of good people,
   and keep to the path of those who obey God's
      standards.

                                                    (2:5-20)

The key to motivating our children is to find a prize they want badly enough. Jenae and Josh, my six- and eight-year-olds, could support the entire General Mills corporation with the amount of Trix®, Franken Berry®, Lucky Charms®, and Cheerios® they eat. The reason for this consumption is not their love for cereal alone. In our family we have a rule—you cannot rifle through the contents of an entire box of cereal in order to find the prize at the bottom. You must eat your way there. Thus, Josh and Jenae spend each morning competing to determine who will get to the bottom first and thus get to keep the prize. Their motivational batteries are on "heavy duty" because they are convinced that the "invisible ink pen" or other plastic gadget will be a priceless treasure. I pray they will have this same intensity to win the rewards of wisdom—intimacy with God (2:5-8), an ability to apply His standards in life (2:9-11), protection from evil men and women (2:12-19), and the enjoyment of God's blessing in life (2:20-22). These rebates are not cheap plastic gimmicks. They are the durable gifts that protect us from breaking.

INTIMACY WITH GOD (2:5-8)

Why should a child pay attention to the advice of Proverbs, memorize and internalize its principles, and cry out to God for insight when he or she doesn't even understand it (2:1-4)? Because obedience to these instructions will give him an exquisite appetite for spiritual values, and he will become hungry for intimacy with the Architect. This closeness with God is both the beginning and end of a life rich in value. He teaches skill to make the right turns, for He is the Author of wise choices. If we stockpile His guidelines, He will give practical competency to meet challenges (2:7). He becomes a shield for us when we sincerely devote ourselves to Him (2:7); He becomes our stronghold (cf. 10:29), guarding and protecting every step (v. 8). Though detested by the wicked (29:27), we will become privy to God's secret counsel (3:32). He will love to hear our prayers (15:8). Consequently, as His devoted worshipers, we can expect security and freedom from anxiety and fear.

DISCERNMENT OF THE RIGHT LIFE PATH (2:9-11)

The Old Testament book of Job wrestles with the agony experienced when, for no earthly reason, bad things happen to good people. Proverbs exposes the truth that good times come to those who choose to obey God's instructions. Perhaps they will not occur until we join Him in heaven, but they *will* come. We must remember Job when we are suffering, but we must not allow our trials to obscure the blessings that come to those who follow God's guidelines. The child who matures in godliness and develops the ability to make accurate decisions as he applies God's truth to life decisions will walk the good path (v. 9). Unlike the moral dullard with his insatiable hunger for foolishness, this child will be attracted to and satisfied by a diet of wisdom (2:10). This correct information will permeate the core of his inner life, where thoughts and feelings mingle to determine choices (4:23). Consequently, they will see through the cheap prizes offered by the demolition crew in chapter 3, and they will choose instead to obey God's morality. This maturity will deliver them from the tragic consequences of unethical behavior.

PROTECTION FROM EVIL (2:12-19)

Those who oppose God are foolish, but they are also cruel and dangerous. God promises to rescue the individual who chooses wisdom from the claws of the criminal who willfully rejects the godly course of life for a path of violence (2:12-15; cf. 4:14-17) and from the talons of the sensualist who abuses sex for selfish gratification (2:16-19). The illicit use of money or sex can be deadly. Since skill in these areas is such a strategic part of wise living we will devote the following chapters to exposing what Proverbs says about these areas. God's kids must stay away from the dark alleys of crime and immorality. Proverbs gives us the facts to help keep our kids safe. But giving them the right information does not guarantee they will make the right choices. Our choices, and theirs as well, express what is actually happening in the core of our personality.

We can choose to walk along God's path with its ever-increasing insight into truth (4:18), or we can choose to stumble along in the darkness of rebellion (4:19). The core of our personality determines the road we take (4:23). This explains God's constant plea "Love Me with all of your heart." We must challenge our children to choose this option.

Parents often come to me and say, "Our child is messed up. He got involved with the wrong crowd. How can we help him to get in with a better group of kids?" In the next chapter we will look at the power of the peer group and learn how to help our kids escape the suction into deadly companionship. However, the question that must first be faced is, "Why do our kids gravitate toward a certain group?"

Kids associate with those who have the same core values they do. Those who desire to love God with all their hearts are drawn to others who have this same desire. Those who live for selfish pleasure and excitement will magnetically attract those with a similar commitment. Unless the naive fool turns his heart wholeheartedly toward God, he will join scoffer, moral dullard, and impenetrable block and will be slain by their waywardness (1:32).

We must challenge our kids to place God at the core of their being, to trust in Him with all their hearts (3:5), and then to guard this commitment as their most vital possession. We must not be afraid to have honest talks about the condition of their hearts or to face the truth about our own hearts. The real internal values of Dad and Mom—not just what we say but who we are—are the most powerful human forces shaping our children's commitments.

As I grew to maturity and began to realize that my parents were not gods or demons but human beings, I had to face the truth—they, too, were sinners. All parents are. My dad often buried himself in his ministry and neglected developing a personal relationship with me. At forty I understand his temptation as I face the pressure of balancing work and family priorities. My mom sometimes talked too much about other people. Though my dad is a prominent Christian leader, neither he nor Mom was perfect. But through the years they were wholeheartedly devoted to their Savior.

I never needed to question the sincerity of their love. Their hearts daily belonged to Jesus. I believe this is the most important factor that explains why all four of my adult brothers and sisters join Dad and Mom in their devotion to the Lord. "Above all else, vigilantly guard your heart, for the impulses that determine one's life flow from this center" (4:23).

Money Blueprints

Use money skillfully to honor Him.
Remember illicit wealth yields death.

5
Bonnie And Clyde

How does a drug pusher influence a teenager? The scenario often begins like this.

"Ben, you've got to come Saturday night! The party is going to be red-hot—beer, music, and knockout, available women. A first-class Saturday night fever!"

How could Ben, a sophomore, turn down an invitation from a senior like Marshall? Marshall's beautiful MG and his girl—the envy of the high school—caught Ben's eye, but he looked down and said, "I could never get clearance from my dad to go to a bash like that."

Marshall shrugged his shoulders. "Don't tell him about the party. I'll have my mom call your parents and invite you to spend the night at our house Saturday. Mom's working, so we'll just take off after she leaves. You've got to come! An old friend of mine will be at the party. He has a perfect way for you to finance that new pickup you want to buy! You won't have to bag groceries twenty hours every week anymore."

Ben was certainly tired of filling brown paper sacks for grocery shoppers, and Marshall's plan worked to perfection. The sophisticated party sent Ben into orbit. From the tips of his toes to the split ends of his hair he had never felt so high. When it was time to leave, Marshall's friend made sure Ben had a few depressants to help him come down.

Several months later Ben was paying for his personal drug needs by selling pills to his friends. His craving for harder stuff eventually meant that he didn't even balk at selling drugs to younger kids. At times he wanted to stop the trip, but by then he knew the names of the wrong people and had seen too many high level deals. A beating after a party and a threat against his parents and kid sister insured that he would remain loyal to the organization.

Why didn't he go to the police? Ben knew that some of the local cops supplemented their low salaries with bribes from his people. Ben found himself tightly wrapped in the multiple arms of the drug octopus.

That octopus sends forth its tentacles to ensnare our kids. One of my closest friends went through the agony of having to ask his own son to leave his home because of his drug dependency. The March 14, 1988 issue of *Time* magazine reported, "Unless drugs are attacked at every level, the U.S. may continue to flail at the problem." Sterling Johnson, a special narcotics prosecutor in New York City, declared sadly, "Every American better just pray each night that we don't lose [the war on drugs]." Then U.S. Education Secretary William Bennett argued that schools cannot be expected to effectively check the demand for drugs when so many youngsters watch their parents feed their own addictions.

Faced with this brutal assault against our country and our children, how should straight parents respond? It will not work to shake our heads and sigh. "It wasn't like this when we were in junior high and high school! Our kids face such sophisticated seductions. How can we hope to counteract the pressure?"

Did parents in biblical times face anything comparable to the drug problem? Popping pills was not the dominant temptation for young people in ancient Israel. But footloose, gold-studded bandits did entice rebellious teens to join their gangs. It was not a little kid's game but the real thing. Life-styles like Butch Cassidy and the Sundance Kid's or Bonnie and Clyde's were "in."

The godly parents of Proverbs do not retreat in bewilderment. They counterattack. They commit themselves to take the time necessary to teach their children the deadly realities of living for illicit highs. They begin the training by saying, "My son, if criminals entice you, strongly refuse them!" (1:10).

PARENTS NOT AFRAID TO SAY NO (1:8-10)

Observe that this dad had moral guts. He didn't sit in his easy chair and hope his son would never face the undertow of the ocean of crime. He didn't lock his son in a monastery to keep him away from evil's deadly pull. Instead, he faced the facts. In the real world his son would most likely be propositioned at some point by the criminal con man. In case of just such an occurrence, he laid down a clear-cut response: "Don't give in!"

PARENTS NOT AFRAID TO ANSWER WHY

How do your young people respond when you lay an authoritative command upon them? Probably with the universal teen challenge, "Why?" How do you respond when hit with this challenge? The authoritarian parent feels threatened and retorts with the basic turnoff, "Because I said so!"

The Bible does teach teenagers to respect and obey their parents (Ephesians 6:1). Rebellious attitudes are sinful even when they occur during the teen years. There are situations when parents can't explain all the reasons for their decisions. But authoritative parents, in contrast to the authoritarians, view the "why" questions as moments of opportunity. These are the charged moments when they can pour street smarts into the minds of their children.

THE CRIMINAL'S BAIT

Using role play as the teaching method, the father lets his son listen to a criminal's sales pitch designed to entice a naive young person to join the gang. Check out Proverbs 1:11-14:

> Come on and join us!
> Let's lie in wait to spill the blood of our victims!
> We'll ambush the unsuspecting innocents!
> Just as death devours life, as certainly as those
>   in the bloom of health can suddenly fall into the
>   pit of death we'll be invincible.

We'll secure all kinds of precious wealth.
We'll fill our houses with plunder.
Throw in your lot with us,
    and we will share a common purse.

Observe this sales talk carefully. Three juicy worms bob enticingly before the prospective catch, and our kids are the victims who could get hooked. What's the bait? *Invincibility, instant wealth,* and *intimacy.* They are still juicy seductions today.

INVINCIBILITY

There is a perverse power in believing that you are an invincible, high-rolling thief and murderer. Think of the movies that have made millions by portraying a swashbuckling hero who blows away anyone and everyone who gets in his way. It's heady to equate yourself with the relentless power of death. We all want to be winners, and the criminal's promise is "Victory—swift and easy! No one will be able to stop you!" He uses the worn-out, ancient line "We'll never get caught."

Though Clyde Barrow stood just 5 feet, 5½ inches tall and weighed barely 127 pounds and Bonnie Parker couldn't edge the scale past 100, with their fingers on the trigger of a Browning automatic rifle (B.A.R.) Bonnie and Clyde were veritable giants. Guess who supplied the Barrow gang with guns and ammunition? On February 19, 1934, they cockily armed themselves courtesy of the U.S. government after burglarizing the National Guard Armory in Ranger, Texas. They miraculously escaped one police roadblock after another and blasted their way out of certain capture.

In the early thirties, the Barrow gang was invincible. Newsboys jumped for joy when the names *Bonnie* and *Clyde* appeared in bold print on the front page. The fame of this elusive couple sold thousands of papers. Bonnie and Clyde seemed invincible, and that invincibility is the first lure in the criminal's persuasive arsenal (1:11).

The second enticing prize is easy money.

INSTANT WEALTH

Why work for money when you can steal it? Like soldiers rummaging through the wealth of a defeated city, the criminal promises "easy pickin's and a quick million."

Just a week after the Barrow gang replenished their arsenal from Uncle Sam's supply, Clyde and his partner, Ray Hamilton, knocked over the bank in Lancaster, Texas. Their women waited in a switch car just south of town. Minutes after the robbery, Ray and Clyde abandoned their original getaway car to be free of the incriminating license plate and sped off with their beauties and the biggest payday yet—$4,433. That kind of money in 1934 could put some respectable threads on anyone's back and buy a lot of pleasure in a distant city. The well-worn criminal line is always, "Who says crime doesn't pay?"

As powerful as the promises of invincibility and instant wealth, they cannot match the firepower of crime's third promise: close friendship.

INTIMATE COMPANIONSHIP

Teens feel a passion to belong to the group. When I was sixteen, I found out just how powerful group influence can be.

I was working at Word of Life Ranch, a children's camp in upstate New York. One of my friends was a first-class womanizer. He not only had a girl at the Ranch, but he also dated a girl at the teenage camp eight miles up the lake, and another at the adult camp. On his days off he would parcel out his time between the two up the lake, and during the week he was with his girl at the Ranch. The key to his success was his beautiful, blond hair, and a group of us decided to remedy the situation.

One night while he was talking with his Ranch girl in the staff lounge, four friends grabbed him. After forcing him into a barber's chair we took shears to his head. Have you ever seen pictures of Mohawk Indians? Then you've got the picture of our former friend's head. But the physical strength of four boys controlling one is not the real power of a group that I observed that night.

The next day at the morning flag-raising ceremony twelve counselors stood behind their line of campers respectfully facing the flagpole with hats on their heads. However, you cannot keep your hat on during the raising of the American flag. When the hats came off, the flag-raising halted. Four hundred campers went into hysterics at all the Mohawk haircuts. You say, "Dave, I thought there was only one haircut that night." That's how many there were at first.

As soon as I put down the clippers that night, the group grabbed me. When my hair was all over the floor someone decided this Mohawk haircut was the "in" thing. Like the plague, one guy after another joined in. When it was over we had a group of more than ten with weird haircuts. Now if you would have asked any of those fellows individually if he wanted his head shaved, except for a strip of hair down the middle, every one of them would have thought you were crazy. But get the group pressure going, and any of us is capable of doing something dumb. Being influenced by the wrong group can get us to do things a lot more stupid than getting a Mohawk haircut.

The criminal knows about the persuasive power of peer pressure. His line therefore becomes an invitation to join the high-rolling set. His gang is where the action is. He seductively smiles and says, "Cast your fate to the wind! Join our free-living life-style! You won't have to fend for yourself. We'll all draw from a common purse. We'll be in this together" (1:14).

Perhaps you saw Hollywood's version of *Bonnie and Clyde*. It received all kinds of critical praise back in the 60s and has been aired on national TV several times since. Who wouldn't be drawn to the love affair between the handsome Warren Beatty and the stunning, youthful Faye Dunaway? While on the run, Bonnie writes beautiful poetry for her Clyde, and they make love in romantic motel settings. Sure, they rob banks, but they throw money to the poor as they escape out of town.

When watching this type of movie, you find yourself admiring the bad guys. Given the opportunity, who wouldn't be tempted to join them? As you are drawn into the movie version of Bonnie and Clyde, the deputies hot on their trail subtly become the enemy, and the thieves and their intimate group of associates become the heroes. But is all that for real? What is the truth about a life of crime?

The parents in Proverbs permit their children to feel the undertow of crime's appeal—invincibility, instant wealth, and intimacy. Then they expose the hard-core truth: crime is cruel, stupid, and self-destructive.

CRIME'S HARD-CORE REALITY

My son, do not associate with them in their lifestyle.
Don't even take the first step down their path of life,
because their feet run to injure their victims.
They eagerly hurry to shed blood.
Surely it is useless to spread out a net
    to trap birds while they watch you set the trap!
But the criminal lies in wait for his own blood.
They ambush their own lives.
Such is the destiny of everyone greedy for unjust gain.
It takes away the life of those who get it.

(1:15-19)

Bandits on television and in movies shoot and kill, but the bloodstained shirts can be easily cleaned. When the director yells "Cut!" the actor jumps to his feet for another scene. The real life bandit, on the other hand, is intoxicated by the blood of his victims. The deadly reality is that he hurries to commit the next murder because of the sheer exhilaration of killing. The yell is not "Cut!" from a movie director but "O God!" from a young widow whose husband has just been blown into eternity.

Stringtown was a quick stopover in southeastern Oklahoma. On Friday evening the biggest thing going in town was the roadside dance. The hottest thing at the dance that night was a whirling, beautiful little blonde in a flaming red dress. Dancing with her two well-dressed male companions, she was the princess of the evening. A local fellow asked the stunning stranger for a dance but was roughly pushed aside by her companions. The moonshine whiskey flowed freely. When the woman and her friends jumped into his car, the rebuffed youth went to the local lawmen for help in removing the outsiders.

Sheriff C. G. Maxwell and his deputy, E. C. Moore, approached the vehicle expecting to investigate a routine misunderstanding. "What's going on here?" Moore asked the strangers. A volley of gunfire was the response, and Moore slumped with a bullet through his forehead. Maxwell fired but was critically wounded by the onslaught of bullets from Bonnie, Clyde, and Ray Hamilton's automatic weapons. This was just one of the cruel murders that bloodied the historical path of the real Bonnie and Clyde. It was a path that left behind eleven murder victims and six others critically wounded.

I pastor a church in Midlothian, Texas, a small town southwest of Dallas. Bonnie and Clyde often used Midlothian as a hideout from the Dallas lawmen. My next-door neighbor, Tommy Hobson, was raised by his grandfather W. A. Parker, Bonnie's uncle. In my living room Tommy shared his impressions of the real Bonnie and Clyde.

"I remember it was late in the evening at my grandfather's home seventeen miles east of Crockett, Texas. I was sitting on my grandmother's lap when a brand-new Model A Ford drove up. The adults suddenly became quiet, and I sensed their fear. Bonnie got out of the car. Clyde nervously waited outside the yard by the gate without killing his engine. Bonnie, a very small woman, approached us. Her hair was all matted. 'We need some food and some help to get down the road!'

"I can still feel the terrible fright in my grandmother as Granddad refused to help. Bonnie's eyes were cold as steel. No one breathed until they roared away.

"Granddad often described Bonnie as a little thing but tough as nails. The kind of woman who could machine-gun you in the face and then spit in the pool of your blood without batting an eyelash."

The street-smart individual will never forget that real crime produces a cold, calloused enjoyment of violence. Violence that yields the horror of a mother's tears at a gravesite and children forced to grow up without their daddy. The irony is that the ultimate victim is the "invincible" murderer himself.

You've heard the expression "You're a real bird brain!" Our kids need to learn that a criminal's common sense makes a bird's brain look like Albert Einstein's.

Dove hunting is popular in Texas. If you have ever done any kind of bird hunting you are well aware of the fact that the hunter does not stand up and shout, "Look here, birdie! Take a peek at my new twelve-gauge!" As the doves fly in to roost, they will abruptly change their flight pattern if they spot you, and you will not get a decent shot.

Ancient Israelites did not use shotguns. Nets provided the means of snaring birds, but the idea was still to not let the birds know what was going on. That's the point of Proverbs 1:17-18. Even a stupid bird knows enough not to get caught in a trap if it sees it. But the criminal is even dumber than a bird. He flies right into his own ambush. When you live by the gun, you die by the gun.

A few months before her death Bonnie wrote these words:

The Story of Bonnie and Clyde

They don't think they're too tough or desperate,
They know that the law always wins;
They've been shot at before,
But they do not ignore
That death is the wages of sin.

Some day they'll go down together;
And they'll bury them side by side;
To few it'll be grief—
To the law a relief—
But it's death for Bonnie and Clyde.

Although they knew the end would be violent death, they kept running until May 1934.

Outside the Majestic Cafe in Shreveport, Louisiana, Bonnie and Clyde waited impatiently for their new young partner, Henry Methvin, to purchase a stack of sandwiches and some soft drinks. Two police officers cruised by. Bonnie and Clyde were sure they had been spotted. Leaving Methvin behind, they took off. Proverbs 28:1 states, "The wicked flee when no one pursues." The police commented later, "We didn't even notice them until they sped away."

Recognizing that the couple might be the desperate duo and that if so they would be outgunned, the Shreveport policemen abandoned their pursuit and reported to their superiors. Back at the cafe Methvin abandoned the sandwich line and quickly left.

Having bloodhounded their trail for two years, Dallas Deputies Bob Alcorn and Ted Hinton knew the habits of Bonnie and Clyde better than those of their own wives. By chance they were in Shreveport when the report about the jumpy couple came in. With Methvin on foot and his father's place about fifty miles east of Shreveport, the deputies knew it was only a matter of time before Bonnie and Clyde tried to pick up their partner at Old Man Methvin's. There was only one graveled road to his place. Just off this road, on a high point commanding a half mile of country road in either direction, Alcorn and Hinton concealed themselves in some underbrush with four fellow officers. Their arsenal of automatic weapons could have blown an oncoming tank off the road. They waited with the mosquitoes and snakes for two days.

At 4:17 A.M. on the second night they heard the familiar cough of Old Man Methvin's Model A Ford truck. The armed police halted him. "What are you doing out this early in the morning? Where's Clyde? Has your son contacted you?"

Methvin cursed and revealed nothing about Bonnie and Clyde's whereabouts. Since he persisted in maintaining silence, the officers took him several feet behind their position and handcuffed the old man to a slender tree.

Turning his truck around, they quickly took off one of the tires and jacked the vehicle up in the middle of the road. Should Clyde drive down this road, the truck would force him to slow. No heavy foot on the accelerator would speed him away this time. The officers had played this game before, and this time they set the bait perfectly before settling back to their vigil. Methvin's father cussed in the background from time to time.

At 9:15 A.M. Hinton heard the sound of a motor. A car sped toward them. *Full speed is the only speed Clyde knows,* Hinton thought. Having grown up in West Dallas with the later-notorious outlaw, Hinton recognized him instantly. "This is it! It's Clyde!" he whispered.

Clyde spotted the truck and slowed. Bob Alcorn stood. "Halt!" His shout shattered the morning. Bonnie screamed, Clyde grabbed for his B.A.R., but like a sheet of rain in a cloudburst, shells struck his weapon rendering it useless. Reaching for a pistol, he tried to get away, but the steel bullets easily penetrated the car and ripped his flesh. Bonnie slumped, her right hand blown off. Fifty-five shells riddled Clyde's body. The mortician later counted fifty in Bonnie. Those who had brought so much grief to others were ambushed in the same machine-gun hell they had created.

Contrary to Bonnie's poetic prediction, they do not lie side by side in a Dallas graveyard. In their book *Ambush: The Real Story of Bonnie and Clyde,* Ted Hinton and Larry Grove quote Mrs. Emma Parker's response to her daughter's request: "Clyde had her for two years, and look what it did for her."

Associating with lawbreakers also caused death three thousand years ago, when the father in Proverbs taught his teenagers. In the thirties the careers of Bonnie and Clyde illustrated the criminal's foolish self-destruction. But can Proverbs 1:10-19 still claim to have a handle on reality today?

I was gathering up my notes after lecturing on this passage at a Bible conference when a middle-aged woman came up to me. "Dave, do you have a minute?"

"Sure! I'm just trying to get these overheads put away."

She hesitated and then went on. "My husband and I were divorced. Our teen-aged son was living with me when he met a new friend at school. I did not like the group this friend ran with, but my negative comments were always met with 'Mom, somebody with his head screwed on right needs to be his friend.' A few times I suspected that this friend was on drugs, but my son was spending more and more time over at his house and less time at home with me."

Her eyes moistened, "One afternoon at his friend's house my son was shot through the head. His friend was high on drugs."

As I weep with this mother, I ask, why this needless waste of lives? Most sports fans remember the 1986 cocaine death of basketball star Len Bias, and my hometown, Midlothian, remembers the brazen assassination of George Raffield, an undercover police officer, by two teenagers. This must cease.

Parents, we must speak with authority to our children about the seduction of drugs. "My son, do not associate with them in their lifestyle. Don't even take the first step down their path of life, because their feet rush to injure their victims!" (1:15). Many of our young people are wising up to the destruction of drugs, but what about sons and daughters already ensnared?

Like the hole in the face of his beat-up guitar Tom knew he was empty. This summer escape from the heat of New York City to the coolness of upstate Lake George was not refreshing his burned-out emotions. He had been a leader in the hippie movement of the sixties. He had spoken of free love and had led demonstrations in Central Park. In reality, however, he was a slave now. Spaced out on drugs, he sat by the lake strumming his guitar.

"Hi, my name is Bruce. Do you mind if I sit down?"

Tom nodded to the college student, and through the fog in his mind tried to make sense of the small talk.

"I'm working at a summer camp for young people named Word of Life," Bruce continued. "Why don't you come up and spend a few days? It'll be a blast. Good food, music, and sports."

Why not? Tom thought. *I'm tired of playing in the streets. A few days of free food and a place to stay before returning to the city would be all right.*

The drugs inside him made the speedboat ride to Word of Life Island seem like he was flying in the clouds. When the men in his cabin introduced themselves as Peter, John, and Paul, Tom thought he had died and gone to heaven. In the meeting that night the message was about how a person could be sure he'd end up in heaven.

Tom heard about Jesus Christ, a divine man who claimed He could give meaning to life. As the evangelist related the simple gospel, Jesus confronted Tom personally with his need for forgiveness. Jesus had died in His place. He claimed to have risen from the dead. Tom knew he had to make a decision concerning who or what he would depend upon. That night he received the Son and became a child of God.

He called his girlfriend in New York City. Vicky came up to see him, and when he explained what Christ had done for him, she too opened her heart to Him. For the rest of the summer they stayed at Word of Life and were strengthened in their relationship with Jesus.

The disciplined reading of the Scripture acted like fresh water cleansing a filthy sponge as Tom and Vicky opened their minds to God. Though they had lived together for more than a year, they broke that intimacy. Freed from drugs and immorality, Tom and Vicky began their college studies that fall. Did the new life last?

After completing their studies and getting married, Tom and Vicky Mahairas moved to New York City to begin a new church. Today Tom is affectionately known by the members of Manhattan Bible Church as Pastor Tom. "For the wages of sin is death but the gift of God is eternal life through Jesus Christ our Lord" (Romans 3:23).

THINK ABOUT IT

1. Parents, what are some areas in which you have set a strong standard of moral discipline? Some areas of weakness? How is this reflected in your children's behavior?

2. Listen to your children's conversation, especially with their friends from school and when they forget you are around. What are some of the "in" groups, according to your teenagers? What kind of influences are these groups having on them?

3. Family discussion: Retell some of the things you have learned from Proverbs 1:8-19. Be careful not to get "preachy." Share some experiences from your own life, and ask your kids to express their views on issues like drugs, night clubbing, and immorality. Listen to them!

4. Pray together as a family, and ask God to give you wisdom and strength to resist the seduction to live for illegitimate wealth and illicit sex. Thank Him for the pure pleasure He alone can give.

6

The Sting

Chet settled down at his desk and opened his English textbook. His first midterm exams loomed one week away. As a freshman he wasn't sure what to expect. At least he had time in the evening to concentrate on his studies and not worry about trying to work a full-time job. All the sweat and strain of working construction for three months the past summer was paying off. He could relax about his tuition for the year. The money was safely waiting in the bank.

Better hit this grammar, he thought, trying to get the study juices going, *or I won't need money to pay for classes!*

He was in the middle of memorizing the definition of "syntax" when two neatly dressed strangers knocked at his dorm room door and immediately entered.

"Hi, the name is Harry. This is my associate, Wilson. Have a few minutes to talk? Fred, next door, got really excited about an opportunity we can make available and said you might be interested in it as well."

Chet glanced at his English text, then at his watch. "It'll have to be quick. Got a test on Monday, and this grammar doesn't stick upstairs easily."

Harry grabbed the other chair in the room, turned it around backwards, and sat facing Chet. "I promise this will take only five minutes. Five of the most valuable minutes you have ever invested." With that his briefcase snapped open, and he began his pitch.

"How many students attend this university? Let's say twenty thousand. Do you know how many pens and pencils they are going to purchase this semester alone? Every single one of them will purchase at least some writing utensils. Why let Bic® and Papermate® make all the money? Imagine how many of your classmates would buy from a fellow student if he offered them a special University edition pen and pencil set at a good price like this one?"

With a flourish Harry opened the elegant box in his hand to reveal his product. Chet had to admit—the fountain pen and matching pencil with the University logo engraved on the side were first-class.

"Chet, these retail for twenty dollars a set. But the unique opportunity for you tonight is that I am prepared to give them to you wholesale for ten dollars. For an initial investment of $800, I'll deliver eighty pen and pencil sets right here to your room. You sell them for twenty dollars and, bingo, you just put eight hundred dollars in your wallet. But this is only the beginning. My company is manufacturing these sets for every university in the state. For every student you are able to recruit to join your business team we will give you five percent of his total sales.

"Do you have a calculator? Suppose you get ten other students to join, and they each sell only the eighty original sets they order. Of course, we are being very conservative. Once your sales team gets a taste of how easy it is to sell this product and the enormous profits they receive, they'll continue to sell far more than the original eighty. But suppose they only sell the first allotment? On the sales of only ten students you make a clear profit of two thousand dollars.

"Chet, this thing could become a gold mine. An organization with forty students selling for you all over the state could make you thousands. Why not get in on the ground floor? Take advantage of this, and in a year you'll be making so much you might debate whether you actually need that college degree to make it big in the business world. Wilson, here, turned down an executive position when he graduated from Princeton. He was making a lot more from the sales organization he built up in college than they offered him in salary.

"We just signed up your friend Fred in the next room. I can see why he's a business major. He seizes windows of opportunity when they come."

Harry pulled Fred's check for $800 dollars out of his wallet. "Chet, tonight you could plant a small seed that would have the potential of growing big bucks for you! Even if you don't have the money saved, why not charge it on your Visa or MasterCard? It's a sure thing. We'll be glad to take either a check or credit card. Which would be better for you?"

Chet looked at the checkbook on his desk then at the open grammar book. "Thanks, Harry, but not tonight. Your five minutes was more like twenty, and I've got to study."

The drug pushing criminal we met in the last chapter is not the only enemy who seeks to seduce our kids into the danger zone of instant wealth. Proverbs also exposes the congenial, smooth-talking "Harry Hustler." A member of the demolition crew (chapter 3), Harry is one manifestation of the moral dullard. He comes with a briefcase full of get-rich-quick stings and bad debts.

THE EXPOSURE OF THE STING

A good-for-nothing, a trouble-maker,
   this is the individual who goes about with a crooked
   mouth,
   who winks his eyes,
   shuffles his feet,
   and signals with his fingers.
His heart twists morality.
Constantly he devises malicious schemes and sows
   strife.
Therefore disaster will overtake him unexpectedly.
In a moment he will be broken, and there will be no
   healing.

(6:12-15)

HIS CHARACTERISTICS (vv. 12-14)

The identifying distinctives of the con man remain remarkably the same across time. We need to alert our kids to his perverted mouth, his deceptive body language, and his malicious schemes so that they will be protected from financial and personal ruin.

Whenever an individual's talk contradicts the financial principles of Proverbs, the red lights will blink on in the mind of the committed and wise individual. He will not succumb to the smooth tongue of the super-salesperson who suggests devious, effortless routes to wealth and fortune (cf. 4:24-27). The Harry Hustlers in life always speak with a "forked tongue." They lie, and our children should not be "babes in toyland" regarding them. We need to teach them about the false advertising, the sting operations, and the high-sounding promises they will encounter in the marketplace. Hustlers twist the truth, and we must train our kids to be on guard against their schemes. They must be wary when promises are too good to be true.

Our children must also be trained to penetrate the hustler's disguise by being alert to his deceptive body language. They must beware of individuals who will not look them right in the eye. In young teens this body language often reveals only a lack of confidence; however, the shifty eyes of the con man indicate not low self-esteem but the treachery of a rotten heart (6:13; 10:10). The eyes are the windows of the soul. Therefore we must teach our children to look people in the eye. When someone cannot meet their gaze with calmness and ease, they should be wary; possibly there are ulterior motives at work.

Harry Hustler's deceptive body language is not limited to his eyes; his feet and hands are also part of his act. When someone is trying to sell you something and he constantly shifts his feet and seems to signal with his hands, proceed with caution. Remember the kid's game "I had my fingers crossed behind my back," which supposedly invalidated what he promised with his mouth? The con artist never grows out of this type of lying. He winks mischievously at his partner as they seek to bait their pigeon. If we train our kids concerning the subtleties of deceptive body language, they will have the skills to avoid being someone's dupe.

Worldly-wise kids are taught that there is an enemy in the marketplace who lies with his mouth, deceives with his body, and uses his mind to constantly carve out malicious scams that harm the unsuspecting (6:14). Parents may inoculate their kids against the masters of intrigue by specifically interacting with their children. They must tell them about the illegality of "chain letters," which promise thousands to the recipient who passes the letter on and sends a few dollars to the addresses in the back. They must warn them of the frauds that periodically plague every business community. These frauds coldly and mercilessly calculate ways to destroy their neighbors (24:8; cf. 11:9; 12:5, 20; 16:27, 30; 21:10). Kids can learn how to counteract such scheming with carefully laid-out plans of their own, which will foster not deception but peace and prosperity (12:20).

HIS PRODUCT (6:14)

The hustler promises a quick, effortless profit, but the bottom line is always the same—*strife*. The con feigns friendship and then abuses the relationship for selfish profit. This trickery generates in its victim an intense desire for revenge that will not easily be quenched (18:19). The resulting quarrels and lawsuits have the explosive power of pulverized charcoal being thrown on glowing embers (26:21). The hustler's end will always be the same. The fox may have pockets lined with money, but the baying hounds will eventually have him treed (6:14).

The individual who lives to make a profit by deceiving others deceives himself in the end. Sudden destruction is Harry Hustler's bottom line. Often his tricks break the law of the land, and he ends up facing the sword of the government (24:21-22). The hustler who refuses to listen to God's warnings will always be cut off by divine retribution, and there will be no one to restore and heal him. In the end no one hustles God.

A few of our kids will face economic ruin because we did not warn them about the hustler's tricks. But far more of them will be seduced by the bondage of easy credit.

THE SLAVERY OF DEBT

The rich rule over the poor, and the borrower is the lender's slave. (22:7)

When I moved to Dallas in the early seventies, it was the invincible city with oil resources piping gallons of dollars into the economy. In the eighties the plummeting price of oil turned off the flow. The entire nation knows of the savings and loan failures, the real estate crashes, and the personal bankruptcies. We have been forced to face the fragility of providing for our daily needs. Jesus did not teach idle words when He taught us to pray, "Give us this day our daily bread."

Our heavenly Father is a gracious provider, but He is also a practical, effective economics professor. We can pray about natural crises that rob our table of food. The graciousness of others in such times of need can get us back on our feet. Bad speculative debts also rob us of necessities, but people are not nearly as willing to rescue us out of holes we dig for ourselves.

To a generation that only asks, "Can I make the monthly payments?" Proverbs has some hard-nosed advice about debt. Wise parents should take the time to share this wisdom with their kids. The mathematics of debt is not advanced calculus, yet few parents give their kids the simple facts about compound interest and the Architect's warning against foolish co-signing and borrowing.

BEWARE! FOOLISH CO-SIGNING
CAN COST YOU THE SHIRT OFF YOUR BACK

> The individual who guarantees to cover the indebtedness of someone he does not know well will suffer for it, but whoever hates to enter into this type of agreement will be secure. (11:15)

> A person lacks common sense who co-signs for another, who assumes legal responsibility for someone else's debts. (17:18)

Proverbs repeatedly warns against pledging to cover another's debt. This is especially foolish when you have not taken the time to discern whether the individual you are certifying is reliable. We need to warn our children about "friends" who beg them to co-sign on the dotted line so that they can procure a loan. Our kids need to remember who will be left with the monthly payments when their friend defaults.

Even worse is the man who gets involved with an immoral woman and then assumes responsibility for her indebtedness. He deserves to lose his shirt (20:16; 27:13). We must talk with our sons about the destructive financial entanglements that result from a romantic involvement with a loose woman. She'll purr in his lap like a kitten, but her claws will tear a hole in his bank account. In chapter 10 we will learn that she robs him of far more than money.

Usually the wise person is cool, calm, and collected. But when he or she makes a mistake and rashly shakes hands on a foolish deal, he must go and frantically pester the individuals involved until he is released from the potentially disastrous obligation (6:1-5).

We must remember—proverbs are not commands but principles that depend upon the circumstances for their application. At times, co-signing a note is a wise and kind course of action. I'm thankful for established business people who gave me the opportunity to begin establishing a good credit rating as a young man. They did not, however, put their basic assets at risk, and they spent the personal time with me necessary to make a judgment about my dependability.

The wise parents of Proverbs had witnessed enough disasters to warn their kids about the hazards of foolish co-signing. On the other hand, they encouraged them to lend freely to legitimate companions and to be generous givers. Though God's children need to be reluctant about assuming responsibility for the debts of others, they need to be quick to lend or give to those in need (14:21; 19:17; 27:10). In the Old Testament God does not allow His children to exact interest from one another when they need money to relieve serious financial difficulty (Exodus 22:25; Leviticus 25:35-37). In the New Testament Jesus instructs us to be willing to lend even to our enemies without expecting repayment. He promises to greatly reward this expression of His Father's merciful generosity (Luke 6:34-35).

Instead of going to the bank and co-signing a note when a fellow believer has a need, why not freely decide how much we can give and expect no repayment? How many brothers and sisters in church families are enemies today because they did not heed this common sense from Proverbs?

Assuming responsibility for someone else's debts is stupid. Losing your freedom because of your own debts is tragic.

BEWARE! DEBT ENSLAVES
(EVEN IN A FREE DEMOCRACY)

> The rich rule over the poor, and the borrower is the lender's slave. (22:7)

Few eighteen-year-olds going out into the world genuinely believe in the power of compound interest. When looking at the sleek lines of a new sports car, few young people consider its actual total cost. Their calculations analyze only whether they can scrape together the $364 necessary to make the monthly payments. Somehow they never look at the objective numbers. A five-year loan to pay for a $16,000 sports car at a periodic interest rate of 1.08 percent will cost $5,843 in interest. The total bill is not $16,000 but $21,843. If he earns $500 a week, he will work 11½ weeks just to pay his lending institution for the privilege of borrowing.

When our kids charge $1,578.01 on a credit card in one year, at a periodic interest rate of 1.67 percent, and make monthly payments totaling $410 for the year, they will still owe $1,255.96 and pay $87.95 in interest. When you consider that the average American family has not one credit card but three or four, you can easily discern how a young couple falls into the credit card trap. We need to help our kids to objectively face the fact that compound interest can work against them.

My dad never sat down and showed me on paper how interest payments escalated. Before the days of computers it was far more difficult to print this kind of data. Today I would encourage all parents to sit down with their children and show them exactly how much interest they will pay when they buy something on credit. This is the negative side of compound interest.

Our children must also be exposed to the power of interest when, instead of borrowing, they are saving. At 8 percent interest a year an initial investment of $10,000 will multiply to $14,898 in five years, $22,196 in ten years, $33,069 in fifteen years, and $49,268 in twenty years. Every financial adviser shows us figures like these.

Few are wise enough to discipline themselves to save regularly. This explains why most families work a good proportion of every year simply paying interest to credit institutions. The math is simple and objective, but the discipline to defer purchases until we can afford them and to save consistently is a priceless skill. Our kids will never learn it unless we parents take a hard look at the figures and at our priorities. Credit is easy, but it creates chains. Saving is difficult, but it leads to power and freedom.

Five weeks after Chet's confrontation with Harry and Wilson, he was again studying at his desk. The "B" on his midterm test was acceptable, but he was beginning to learn the system, and an "A" was not out of reach in the next round. There was a knock at his door.

"Chet, can I come in for a minute?"

"Sure, Fred. How are things going?"

"Not too well. Remember those executive types who came through the dorm about a month ago?"

"Yea, they told me you got in on the ground floor of a great profit-making bonanza. Let me see one of the pen and pencil sets they sent you."

Fred grimaced. "That's what I came to ask you about. They cashed my check, but I never received a thing. I called the number on their business card, and they never heard of any Harry with a pen and pencil business. Do you have any ideas about how I can get my $800 back? I need it to stay in school next semester."

THINK ABOUT IT

A business professor shared how a sharp enterpriser earned a bundle when everyone was thinking about solar energy. He took out an ad in the major papers: "Solar Dryer—just $48.98! Everything you need!"

He included a post office box number, and the checks and orders poured in. The people received their order, much to their chagrin—a clothesline and pins worth about $3. Nothing illegal was done, and the entrepreneur made a killing.

Using the principles learned in this chapter, discuss with your family whether that idea would be good to implement. Why or why not?

7

The Sluggard

Saturday morning our garage was in chaos, an eloquent testimony to the Second Law of Thermodynamics. The time had come to inject some energy into the system and move it back from the brink of total disorder, so I began sweeping and shoveling the dirt. In their room my two teenage sons slept until late in the morning, then sat around reading.

Sneezing and inhaling the mushroom cloud of dust, I thought about my two strong, young men cooling it inside. "Jonathan and Joel, you should know I need your help," I murmured to myself. "Kids! Mention a good time—they're pulsating with energy. Face them with a dirty garage—they need their sleep."

My anger began to boil as I cleaned alone. "If they can't see what needs to be done, it's not worth asking them!"

At the critical point I slammed the broom to the floor and rushed inside. "Did you guys ever think I might need some help?" I grabbed another Kleenex® and sneezed. "All you do is think about yourselves." This onslaught of verbal gunfire strafed them in total surprise.

Later that day when I had cooled down, I went to them and apologized. When you are growing six or eight inches every few months and your week is a complex juggling act of balancing athletics, piano practice, homework assignments, and church youth group activities, you do need extra sleep. Jonathan and Joel were not maliciously taking advantage of me. I needed to remind myself that the person who internally seethes but refuses to directly ask others for help will spend his entire life doing things alone.

It is a medical fact that young people need more sleep than adults. Parents must put this constant into the equation for raising them wisely. On the other hand, we must also recognize that the individual who sleeps daily until 10:00, becomes an expert on game shows and soap operas, spends the afternoon in a cafe drinking coffee and spinning yarns with his buddies, and boasts about all he is going to accomplish is becoming enslaved to laziness. Proverbs exposes the disposition and destiny of Sam Sluggard. We can humorously laugh at his antics, but our kids must be alerted to the paralyzing consequences of becoming a "couch potato."

Two Cartoons

The lazy man does not roast his game, but diligence is a man's precious wealth. (12:27)

The lazy man buries his hand in the dish. He is too tired to return it to his mouth. (26:15; cf. 19:24)

With satire the writer of Proverbs first pictures the sluggard as a lethargic hunter. Even if he does muster the energy to bag his game, he runs out of gas before a proper fire is kindled and his game is roasted. In contrast to the diligent individual, he never tastes the succulent rewards of his success. He's too lazy to cook his own meat.

The second verbal cartoon takes us to an oriental meal. Instead of sitting on chairs at a table, the custom in ancient Israel was to recline on the floor and dip into a common dish. Visualize a group of teens eating chips and dip on your living room floor while watching videos, and you've got a good approximation to the scene of Proverbs 19:24. Sam Sluggard is so lazy he falls asleep with his hand in his dish. Everyone snickers as French onion dip oozes between his listless fingers. In the midst of the laughter, Proverbs provokes us to take a serious look at ourselves and evaluate how many of the termites of laziness are already eating away at our life structures.

THE LAZY DISPOSITION

The couch potato detests work, but he loves to sleep, talk, dream, and make excuses.

DANGEROUS SLUMBER

If you expect to harvest, you must plant. If you expect to reap success, you must plant the seeds. The wise son plants his seeds. The lazy son disappoints his father by sleeping through the planting season and missing the moment of opportunity (10:5). At harvest time, filled with optimism, he expects to share the rewards with the sowers. But crops will not grow from his unsown ground (20:4). Intelligence, talent, and opportunity do not yield success while he pulls up the covers and rolls over in bed like a door on a hinge (26:4). The father's admonition is simple but strong: "Do not love sleep, lest you be reduced to penury; open your eyes, and you will eat well" (20:13).

Those words convict me at 5:45 A.M. when I am tempted to hit the snooze button on the clock radio. *Fifteen more minutes of precious relaxation, the most cherished sleep of the night,* I say to myself. A swift kick from Mary jars me to reality. "It's time to get up and get planting."

Our children must be trained to respond to alarm clocks. If they do not, someday it could cost them their jobs. Companies tolerate only so many tardy slips. How many college degrees have been forfeited simply because a student consistently did not get up to the alarm? "The door turns on its hinges, the sluggard turns over in his bed" (26:14).

EMPTY TALK

When the sluggard is awake, instead of working, he is gabbing. His mouth is filled with exciting stories about what he is going to do. There is nothing wrong with Sam's appetite for prosperity. He covets the rewards hard work can bring. What he lacks is the will to work hard (13:3-4). Consequently, the frustration of unfulfilled longings will be the death of him (21:25-26). In chapter 15 we will face the awesome power of words, but words are impotent when they are not connected to a person's feet. "In all hard work there will be abundant profit, but mere talk brings nothing but need" (14:23).

IMPOSSIBLE DREAMS

When you first meet Sam Sluggard, he impresses you with the dazzling array of opportunities that await him. If athletics claims his interest at the moment, you will hear of his past victories and the million-dollar professional contracts he could sign. If the conversation turns to business, he becomes the erudite stockbroker with inside tips for investing and cunning strategies for marketing a new product. He is an expert on everything. If you don't believe it, ask him (26:16).

This explains why Sam cannot keep a job. His employers never appreciate his worth to the company, he claims. Often he must quit because another dream has beckoned. This is the "big one" he's been waiting for all his life. In desperation, his family follows him from one place to another as he pursues his impossible dream. In reality, the dream is a nightmare as he flees his creditors.

Proverbs is not demeaning the importance of dreams, especially for the young. A friend of mine, Tonya Crevier, is barely five feet tall. As a teenager she dreamed of becoming a basketball player. Everyone mocked this short girl's goal, but, unlike the sluggard, her talk was not mere fantasy. She practiced for hours on her ball handling and shooting. She developed an incredible ability to spin a basketball on her finger tips. Her skills at ball handling and passing enabled her to star in high school and college ball. Today she earns her living spinning basketballs for thousands during NBA halftimes as one of the world's preeminent ball handlers. Proverbs speaks not against dreams but against a failure to develop one's available resources.

> The one who works his ground will be satisfied with bread, but the person who chases fantasies lacks any sense. (12:11)
>
> They will be filled with poverty. (28:19)

These Proverbs present more than common sense for farmers. God gives all of us a plot of ground—our talents. We must cultivate our potential by discipline and practice. Laziness is not a joke. It is the sinful failure to invest our God-given abilities and use them to be productive for Him. Laziness buries that precious bag of gold in a hole of wild excuses. The Creator's anger burns against this waste (Matthew 25:14-30).

PARALYZING FEARS

When you ask the couch potato why he did not go out and check out the "help wanted" classified leads you cut out of the Sunday paper for him, he replies, "There is a lion outside, I could be murdered in the middle of the marketplace" (22:13; cf. 26:13).

Wild excuses and irrational fears throw a pretense of legitimacy over the sluggard's failure to get going and find a job. His excuse was actually more farfetched in ancient Israel than it would be in our society. Lions did prowl the land but not on crowded streets. However, drugs, muggings, the hazards of driving on the freeway, and a bad economy represent the "lions" of the modern world that your lazy offspring, relative, or friend might use to explain why he cannot go out and hunt for work. He will, however, allow *you* to go out in the danger zone to put bread on the table and a roof over his head. Wild excuses are the trademark of laziness.

THE PRODUCTS OF LAZINESS

Laziness produces undependability, restricted options, and finally enslaving poverty. "Like vinegar setting the teeth on edge, or smoke stinging the eyes, so is the sluggard to those who send him to fulfill a responsibility" (10:26).

In contrast to the reliable individual who brings refreshment to those who trust him because he carries out responsibility, the sluggard produces agony for those who depend upon him. His job never gets completed. He procrastinates, makes wild excuses, and gets distracted. Like the hare in the fable, he falls asleep in the clover patch while the dependable tortoise faithfully wins the race. "The way of the sluggard is like a hedge of thorns, but the path of the upright is an unimpeded highway" (15:19).

Laziness causes one to throw away the opportunities of youth, thus leading to restricted options in adulthood. Bad grades in high school limit the couch potato's options for college. Partying and oversleeping in the first semester of community college yield probation slips and expulsion after finals. Powerful friends provide a well-paying labor job for their lazy, young friend. They feel sorry for him and give him an opportunity. He needs time to mature and get his feet on the ground, they say. But after showing up late for his shift three times and then asking the boss for vacation time, he returns to his room at Dad and Mom's jobless. Sponging off his parents protects him for a time from being beaten up by the villain of poverty (6:10-11).

God graciously cares for those trapped in poverty by ill health, natural disaster, or other tragic circumstances. He commands His children to be generous to the needy (14:21, 31). On the other hand, God does not say those who refuse to follow the example of the ant and work hard to provide for themselves (6:6-8) or those who neglect to cultivate their abilities and sow their opportunities (24:32-34; 20:5) deserve to be fed. Paul remembered this practical advice when he counseled the Thessalonians about idlers, busybodies, and moochers: "If anyone will not work, neither will he eat" (2 Thessalonians 3:10). Hunger is one teacher who might be able to get through to Sam Sluggard and arouse him from his deadly slumber.

If lazy tendencies continue, the sluggard will lose his freedom to enslaving poverty (10:4; 12:24). Before our kids submit to such bondage, we must give them the cure for lethargy.

THE CURE FOR SLUGGARD'S DISEASE

The parent following the learn-and-live model of parenting knows that intense exposure to reality is a major factor in communicating values. If children are lazy, they need to see the effects of laziness fleshed out in life. The previous section contains common sense ideas. The problem with common sense, however, is that we assume everyone has it, so we don't bother to spell things out clearly for the younger generation. We must raise our children in homes where Sam Sluggard is viewed as a dangerous thief who desires to rob them of their talents and opportunities (6:10-11).

They do not have to be enslaved by irrational fears. They can commit their efforts to the Architect and know that He will bring everything to a successful conclusion (16:3, 9). This confidence provides the motivation to diligently plan and pursue goals (10:4; 14:23; 21:5). With trust in the Lord we can develop our available resources. He can teach us priorities—to be willing to put off the consumption of wealth until the means for generating wealth have been put into place. You do not go out and mortgage a house and then go looking for a job (24:27). God can teach His child diligence as he learns to observe the bustling activities of His tiny creatures, such as ants and bees (6:6-8).

A mother screams at her kids about their clothes thrown all over the room but continues to pick them up. A dad angrily demands that his twenty-four-year-old son move out of the house and find a job but continues to make payments on his son's sports car and gas credit card. Such parents are like the devoted family member who feels sorry for the paraplegic in the family and, therefore, does everything for him. Only the therapist, who gets tough and makes the paraplegic learn what he can do for himself, loves that paraplegic. The couch potato needs to be fried—he must experience the painful effects of his laziness. Only then will he be willing to enter the school of diligence and industry.

My garage is filthy again. It's time to wake up Jonathan, Joel, Joshua, and Jenae. We can make a family project of overcoming the chaos by some diligent sweeping.

8

Skillful Money Management

So if you have not been trustworthy in handling worldly
wealth, who will trust you with true riches? (Luke 16:11;
NIV).

We can warn our kids against the seduction of the criminal
gang, the tricks of the sting, and the sluggard's deadly slumber, but
they cannot graduate from the Wisdom School of Finance until they
know the value of the dollar, the threats it can bring, and the meaning of shrewd management of their heavenly Daddy's dollars.

THE VALUE OF MONEY

With hard-headed realism, Proverbs answers the question,
"How much is our money worth?" Some security, some friends,
and some power.

SECURITY

The wealth of the rich is their fortified city, but the terrifying ruin
of the poor is their poverty. (10:15)

Who has more serenity when the bills arrive in the mail-
box—the individual with thirty thousand dollars in CDs tucked
away in the bank, or the individual who already used all of next
week's paycheck to make the minimum payments on his credit
cards? Landing in a hospital bed causes trauma for everyone. But

fears greatly increase when you cannot afford health insurance. To live from one week to the next worrying about how to feed your family is frightening. The next meal is hardly a concern for the wealthy. Proverbs' point is obvious: poverty brings terror, and a savings account provides some sense of security. Proverbs goes on to tell our kids the whole truth—wealth does bring a measure of security, but it is never secure. It can be attacked by circumstances beyond one's control, sprout wings, and fly away (18:11; 23:5).

When the oil crisis struck Houston, high-rolling yuppies, living in posh, upper-class neighborhoods, went into their bankers' offices and laid the keys to their homes and their Cadillacs® on the desk. With no jobs, how could they continue making their payments? Money can never give us a piece of the Rock. God alone is an impregnable Gibraltar. The wise individual trusts in Him and finds a durable security.

FRIENDS

> The poor man is hated even by his companions, but those who love the rich are many. (14:20)

The friend who never has enough money to pick up his own tab at a restaurant but expects you to cover for him will not be your friend for long. The tendency to mooch off the generosity of others destroys one's opportunity to develop healthy, mature relationships. Even members of your family begin to dread your appearance when you always come with your palm up (19:7). Our children need to be taught to pay their own way.

At times friends will graciously pay the bill, and we need to receive this with thankfulness. We must, however, warn our children against expecting this. As a pastor this was an important lesson for me. Closeness with others cannot be built if you constantly expect them to give you special treatment because you are a minister. Pastors who ask for their clergy discount, discount their reputation in a community. We must all learn the art of knowing when to carry someone else's burden, when to allow someone else to carry ours, and when to carry our own (Galatians 6:2-5).

Though chronic need is a friendship repellent, money in the wallet attracts a crowd. If you have a box at the stadium and invite others to the games, if you can afford to pick up the tab at fancy restaurants, and if you can pay for others to accompany you on exotic vacations, you will not lack for company. Jesus Himself taught us to win friends with generosity, graciously forgiving debts and using money to meet the needs of others (Luke 16:9-10). Because the ultimate Master loves to cancel debts, the individual who reflects this divine characteristic will be welcomed into his eternal home (Luke 16:10). The individual who manipulates people will face the opposite destiny.

Money does win friends and influence people. But what kind of friends does it win? If you're wealthy, the threat is that access to your money, rather than true desire for participation in your life, can become the basis of relationships. The prodigal son learned in the school of hard knocks that when the cash is gone, so are the companions. Alone, we discover we have been used, not loved.

POWER

"The rich rule over the poor" (22:7*a*). Money is power. Proverbs tells it like it is. The wealthy make the investments, set the interest rates, and lobby the government. The poor individual must become an expert in using words to win the favor of their benefactors. The powerful rich brusquely say whatever they please without worrying about how it will be taken (18:23). On the other hand, the affluent often forget there is an ultimate Judge who is not impressed with their money (11.4, cf. James 1.10-11). Money has value, but not in the end. Wisdom is practical: wealth has some worth, but there are nine possessions money cannot buy.

VALUES MORE VALUABLE THAN MONEY

My brother Ron is three years younger than I. I remember as kids carrying on intense negotiations together over money. On his birthday he would open a card from one of our relatives, and a dollar bill would be tucked inside. Opportunity knocked for his "worldly-wise" eight-year-old brother. Holding a shiny dime in his face, my line would begin, "Ron, it's too bad they just gave you a piece of paper. Wouldn't you rather have this nice, shiny money? It will last much longer. Look! You can't tear it. Since it's your birthday, I'll trade you even."

My five-year-old brother would take the dime every time. His naivete about the value of money enabled me to cheat him until Dad and Mom discovered my duplicity and put an end to my hustling career. Our children will lose far more than a dollar bill if we fail to teach them nine values in life that are worth more than money:

1. WISDOM

Always choose wisdom over money because it can give you a long, pleasant life and the ability to generate prosperity (3:13-18). When our teenagers want to work long hours at a fast-food restaurant to pay for a new pickup and their report cards drop below passing, we need to talk with them concerning whether they are trading dollars for dimes. Their options in the sophisticated modern marketplace will be limited if they waste their opportunity to get an education (8:10-11; 16:16).

2. RIGHTEOUSNESS

Always choose obedience to God's standards as revealed in His Word over money. When He evaluates our lives, moral character, not money, will be vital (11:4). Materialism offers no reliable bank and trust. God alone is worth our trust (11:28). The person who pursues wealth bankrupts his soul eternally (Luke 12:13-21). The person who hungers and thirsts for conformity to God's standards ends up walking on exactly what the wealthy lived their lives for, for gold is the gravel of heaven. "Blessed are those who hunger and thirst for righteousness, for they will be filled" (Matthew 5:6; NIV).

3. REVERENCE

Always choose to revere the Lord rather than to make a profit. When money becomes god, trouble becomes a way of life (15:16). If we adore God, we end up gaining wealth, honor, and life (22:4).

4. LOVE

Always choose genuine closeness with others over lavishly gratifying your physical desires. Eating Cheerios with loved ones who care is better than eating prime rib with those who hate you (15:17). In my third year of college I was a newlywed, and I remember eating saltines and peanut butter because our money for the month was gone. But Mary's love turned saltines into steak. We all know money cannot purchase love. If we have love, we are far richer than the one who only has money. Ultimately, the person who receives God's love has both love and prosperity (21:21).

5. HUMILITY

Always choose to build your sense of value on the fact that you are made in God's image, rather than on the pretense that the possession of money makes you worth something. When faced with the choice to high-roll it with the proud, "self-made" materialists or be oppressed with those who possess only moral and spiritual values, choose the humble team. This is God's team, and His team always wins (16:18-19). Moses knew this and became immortal (Hebrews 11:26-27). Like the righteous lovers, the humble receive even wealth in the end (22:4). "Blessed are the meek, for they will inherit the earth" (Matthew 5:5; NIV).

6. PEACE

Always choose peace over prosperity. Eating crusty, old bread in peace and quiet is better than banqueting in splendor with hostility and strife. The gleam in the glamorous festivities of the rich is often the glint of steel off a hidden dagger, which will cut your throat (17:1). Those who live for power and prestige produce discord, not harmony. "Blessed are the peacemakers, for they will be called the sons of God" (Matthew 5:9; NIV).

7. INTEGRITY

Always choose to remain ethically blameless rather than becoming rich through illicit means (19:1; 28:6). Remaining spiritually sound is more valuable than causing your entire personality to become diseased because you cheated to get rich. "Blessed are the pure in heart, for they will see God" (Matthew 5:8; NIV).

8. TRUTHFULNESS

Always choose to be an honest poor man rather than a rich liar (19:22). Our lives need to model dependability. Many say, "You can count on me," but few mean it (20:6). When things get tough, the unfaithfulness of the liar hurts more than an abscessed tooth (25:19). Our children need to be taught to place a high price tag on the truth.

9. REPUTATION

Always choose to maintain a good name instead of a large bank account (22:1). Our character gives us far more weight in a community than our money. The chieftains of the Colombian drug cartel can use their money to build massive mansions in Medellin, with manicured lawns and helipads, but their dirty money cannot purchase a good name.

Esteem is priceless and delicate. Our kids need to face reality. A reputation built throughout a lifetime can collapse in a moment. President Nixon's name is synonymous with Watergate, not with the opening of relations with China. Even a child is building a name for himself, either good or bad (20:11). Jesus' actions as a boy won Him favor with God and man (Luke 2:52). In collecting funds the apostle Paul maintained proper accounting procedures to guard against any criticism (2 Corinthians 8:21). A good reputation with outsiders—not the giving power of the donor—was the first qualification of leadership in the first-century church (1 Timothy 3:2, 7).

Choices are not complicated in Proverbs, but they are critical. Whenever our kids face the decision of choosing between wisdom, righteousness, reverence, love, humility, peace, integrity, truthfulness, or reputation and money, they need to place the higher price tag on the former values. To not do so is greedy, worshiping things instead of kneeling before our Creator (Ephesians 5:5). Greed brings nothing but trouble (15:27). By displaying proper values in our own lives we can train our children not to trade dollars for dimes.

THE HAZARDS OF MONEY

Advertisers trigger our children's dreams about all the fun their products can bring. Who challenges kids to stop and think about some of the hazards that accompany all the "stuff" money can buy?

Have they considered that with affluence comes threats from thieves, kidnappers, and blackmailers? Of course, the rich can afford Doberman guard dogs, alarm systems, impenetrable walls, and locked iron gates to protect their estate from enemies. Should they be kidnapped, they can pay the ransom. On the other hand, a poor man doesn't need an alarm system. Who wants to bother with extorting money from one who has none? (13:8). When there's nothing to lose, who cares if you lose it? Few stop and consider that there are advantages to being poor.

Making money is a life-threatening addiction. The love of money places the individual on the "just one more dollar" treadmill, a stress test that will not turn off until your heart collapses. We need to warn our kids against destroying their health while trying to make it big (23:4). Just when you think you have it made, the stock market crashes, and you have to begin the climb all over again. When you reach the top and finally begin to enjoy being king of the mountain, you notice shortness of breath—an arteriogram reveals clogged arteries. All the stress generated the wrong kind of cholesterol. Bypass surgery prolongs your life for a while, but eventually your pumper gives out, and you leave everything behind to worthless relatives who never sweated a day in their lives (Ecclesiastes 5:13-17).

We need to pray with our children for the golden mean: "Give us today our daily bread." Too little bread, and we can be driven to steal, thus shaming our God. Too much bread, and pride can cause us to say, "Who needs God?" (30:7-9; cf. Job 21:13-16). There are no self-made men or women. Worldly-wise kids understand the three hazards of money worship—the threat of kidnap, the threat of physical collapse, and the threat of spiritual collapse. On the positive side, they need to learn how to spend their heavenly Daddy's money wisely.

PRIORITIES IN USING OUR HEAVENLY DAD'S MONEY

"David, here's my wallet," my dad would say. "Ride your bike downtown, and pick up a loaf of bread and a gallon of milk for Mom."

I still remember the pride I felt feeling Dad's thick, leather wallet stuffed with bills—to a ten-year-old, fifteen ones seemed like a fortune—against my right thigh, safe in my pocket. One couldn't be too careful about pickpockets. I was also careful to use only the exact amount required for the grocery purchase. The fact that Dad trusted me with his wallet meant a great deal to me. This trust resisted the temptation to buy a big Baby Ruth or one of the model airplanes that beckoned from the craft store. When we grow up we must realize that a greater Father entrusts us with His resources. We will get our priorities in purchasing right when we realize our heavenly Daddy has entrusted us with His wallet. In order of importance here are four guidelines that have helped me to spend God's money God's way.

1. HONOR HIM WITH MONEY (3:9-10)

Once a year at income tax time we all have to prepare a thorough accounting of our money for the government. Go into your files and retrieve last year's readout of expenditures. Carefully observe where your money was spent. This gives an objective indication of the things that are important in your life. More important than percentages, Proverbs teaches us to esteem God with every dollar. We must not give him 10 percent and then feel free to do with the rest whatever we please since we have paid our dues. An accountant should be able to look at our entire budget and conclude that God is given weighty consideration in our life (3:9-10). Where we invest our treasure indicates the true location of our heart (Luke 12:34).

From the toddler stage, our children should be trained to give to help relieve the hard times of fellow Christians as an expression of their love for God (1 John 3:16-18; 2 Corinthians 8:9, 13). They must be taught to tangibly honor the importance of the gospel by supporting those engaged in the ministry of spreading His Word (Galatians 6:6). Their giving should be consistent and in proportion to God's provision for them (1 Corinthians 16:2; 2 Corinthians 9:6). We need to challenge them to think, *How can I honor God with my allowance?* When they begin to work, they can continue to value the Lord in their giving.

2. MEET THE MATERIAL NEEDS OF YOUR FAMILY

Credit cards should not be used to fake a higher life-style than you can afford when there is not enough money to pay for necessities (12:9; 13:7). The wise individual settles down, earns the bread he eats, and lives within his means (2 Thessalonians 3:12). God places a high value on meeting the needs of one's family (1 Timothy 5:8). The good man values these money management principles; therefore, he is usually blessed far beyond his simple necessities. His savings bring benefit even to his grandchildren (13:22).

3. GRACIOUSLY GIVE TO THOSE IN NEED

The wise person does not feed couch potatoes, but he does feed those who are suffering in poverty (14:21). Generosity to the needy honors the Lord. The individual who pridefully insults the poor and increases their oppression will face the anger of their Defender (14:31).

Joshua, my second-grader, revealed some of the values he was adopting in this spelling piece he did for school: "If I were a farmer, I would plant wheat for my crop. I would use it to make bread to feed the birds and me. I would sale it to rase money for my stuff. I would give some of my money and food that I rase to the poor people. And to rusia."

We are continuing to work with Josh on the peculiarities of English spelling—things are always not as they sound. But, unlike the rich farmer in Jesus' story who only stored up his "stuff" for himself (Luke 12), I am glad Joshua wants to give to meet the needs of others, including the Russians.

4. ENJOY WITH OTHERS
THE GOOD THINGS GOD GIVES YOU

Because of God's kindness, those who follow the practical values of working hard and living within their means normally accumulate more than enough to meet their necessities. We honor God not only by giving to the poor and to those who proclaim His Word but also by using our abundance to bring joy to others. God alone can give satisfaction, which is the ability to enjoy the fruit of hard work (Ecclesiastes 2:24-25; 5:18-20; cf. 1 Timothy 6:17-19). Godly parents warn against both the pride of possessions and the pride of privation. Neither opulence nor asceticism pleases our heavenly Daddy. He wants us to use the money in His wallet to honor and enjoy Him and to meet our own needs and the needs of others.

Sex Blueprints

Cherish the intoxication of marital love;
hate the deception of illicit sex.

9

The Sex Teacher

If you have a teenager, you're accustomed to the perpetual ring of a telephone. The calls to our house used to be for me or my wife. Now the phone rings, and the caller says, "Hello, is Jonathan there?"

At sixteen Jonathan is my eldest, a sophomore. The call is from a good-looking high school girl, two years older than he. What happened to the days when the fellows did the calling and the pursuing? The frequent calls send shock waves not through his system but through mine. He listens to his mother's advice that any girl worth getting to know won't throw herself at him. My emotional reaction to the reality that my son is now taller than I am and definitely attracting attention from the opposite sex is, "Perhaps I should lock him up in a monastery for the next six years. The temptations in today's marketplace are tough!"

John Hopkins University Professors Melvin Zelnik and John F. Kramer indicate that nearly 50 percent of the nation's 10.3 million young women between the ages of fifteen and nineteen have had premarital sex (*Newsweek*, September 1, 1980).

In a 1987 article, "What's Gone Wrong with Teen Sex," *People* magazine exposed the extent of promiscuity among high school students. "In America 3,000 adolescents become pregnant each day. A million a year. Four out of five are unmarried. More than half get abortions, 'Babies having babies.' Or killing them" (April 13, 1987).

Our teenagers face incredible social pressure. Virginity is a "dirty little secret," and the "responsible" way to stop the AIDS crisis is to use condoms, and sex is OK if done with someone you care about deeply. This promiscuous atmosphere pressures us to react, and it is tempting to resort to the monastery approach. But again, as in dealing with the enticement to take drugs, no walls are massive enough to insure against the penetration of immorality. *The rigid, threatened approach could also rob our children of the free expression of sexual passion God intends for them to enjoy in marriage.*

Some evangelical parents confidently say, "This adolescent promiscuity is a problem for the secular humanists. Our kids are safe within the walls of sound, Bible-believing churches and Christian schools. Let's keep quiet about sex, and maybe our teens will innocently escape the magnetism of lust."

Sadly, this is never the case. I went to a Christian high school buried in the depths of orange groves in central Florida. We saw the outside world for a couple of weeks at Christmas and then not again until summer. This isolation did not prevent immorality from infecting some of my classmates.

Because I do about fifteen hours of pastoral counseling each week, I frequently come into contact with Christian girls who are illegitimately pregnant or "born again" guys who admit that they cannot control their sexual passion. The statistics concerning immorality in the church are not significantly different from those in the secular world. The recent fall of some of the most outspoken defenders of sexual purity should caution anyone against believing he or she can escape to a place of safety, free from the threat of lust.

There is evidence to suggest, however, that some adults are wising up about immorality. A desire for intimacy, the secure fulfillment of faithful family living, and the reality that AIDS is not an itch but death, have caused the rebels of the sixties to become the conservatives of the nineties. *Time* magazine declared in 1984 that "The Revolution Is Over" and made this conclusion: "Most Americans seem stubbornly committed to family, marriage and the traditional idea that sex is tied to affection or justified by it. 'Cool sex,' cut off from the emotions and the rest of life, seems empty, unacceptable, or immoral."

The movie *Fatal Attraction* made big bucks from the collective guilt of an adult generation that is learning that a one-night stand could be murder. But are teenagers tuning in to this newfound wisdom? The sexual health of the next generation depends upon our teenagers hearing the right sex educator, a communicator with the courage to expose the tragedy of sexual immorality and the ecstasy of passionate sexual fulfillment in marriage.

THE PREEMINENT SEX EDUCATOR

Parents blush, Dr. Ruth chatters on, and the guys in the locker rooms continue to boast about their exploits. Listen to some of the advice offered to teenagers from today's sex experts. When asked about the AIDS crisis, eminent John Hopkins sexologist Dr. John Money gave this solution: "What we should be doing as a society is giving very explicit and strongly positive messages to young people getting ready for puberty on the positive joys of masturbation . . . not general instruction, but very explicit teaching" (*Psychology Today,* May 1988). He blames our sexual problems on archaic religious ideas. The old morality, he claims, restricts scientists like himself from teaching the truth about sexual freedom.

I agree that religious tradition has often repressed legitimate sexual desire, but treating human sex as primate mating behavior is not the answer either. In the midst of the cacophony of advice, the father and mother of Proverbs offer the truth about healthy sexual behavior. Their instructions go far beyond biology to the crucial issue of how to motivate children to live morally. Here we find parents who accept their sex education responsibility, who know the divine truth about sexual behavior, and who seek to entice budding adolescent sexual desires toward wisdom, not foolishness. Their three sex talks begin with confidence:

> Son, pay attention to my wisdom,
> Open your ears to my understanding,
> That you may follow well-considered sex practices
> And that your lips may guard knowledge.

> (5:1-2)

My son, observe your father's commandment
And do not abandon your mother's teaching!
Continually bind them upon your heart.
Clasp them around your neck.
Wisdom will guide you when you walk.
She will watch over you when you lie down.
She will speak to you when you awake.
For this commandment is a lamp
And this teaching is light.
The way of life is found by heeding corrective
discipline that will protect you from the evil woman,
from the smooth tongue of the woman of mystery.

(6:20-24)

My son, obey my words!
Treasure my commandments within you!
If you obey my commandments you will live.
Guard my instructions as the apple of your eye.
Bind them on your fingers.
Write them upon the tablet of your heart.
Say to wisdom, "You are my sister!"
Call understanding your intimate friend.
They will protect you from the sensual woman,
From the mysterious woman with her seductive words
of flattery.

(7:1-5)

THE PARENTAL RESPONSIBILITY

Who needs a recent poll from *Time* to know that parental apathy is a major factor in creating the present "values vacuum"? More than 90 percent of those who responded to a *Time* survey agreed that morals have fallen because parents fail to take responsibility for their children or to imbue them with decent moral standards (May 25, 1987). We parents know that a social worker, guidance counselor, or pastor cannot replace us as the initial teachers concerning sexual relationships. The difficulty is getting the right message across to our kids.

When reminded of our responsibility to talk to our children about sex, we tend to overreact. Painfully aware that our passion to get ahead of the Joneses often robs us of involvement in our kids' personal lives, we try to make up for lost time by delivering stern lectures. Dads especially love to be preachers. But the "preachy" mode is a turnoff for our children.

The scene begins with Dad's getting out his podium, dusting off the family Bible, sitting his kids down in orderly rows, and then eloquently delivering sermon number 46, "Sexual Purity." He forgets that the kids were looking forward to going out for pizza with their friends. Noticing their bored restlessness, he concludes that the younger generation has no interest in spiritual values.

The wise parents in Proverbs take a different tack. They did not begin with a sermon but with a relationship. They took the time to be personally involved in their son's life. Years later when he committed their teaching to writing, he reminisced about his childhood and concluded, "I was a son to my father, tenderly loved and unique in the heart of my mother" (4:3).

Here was a dad who did more than create a child. He fathered a son. He gave himself to his child. He invested the personal time the father-son relationship demands.

Here was a mom who affectionately treated each of her children as an individual. She made each feel he was one-of-a-kind by the tender way she loved him.

Nothing is more important than time in building a relationship. Time to listen on the way to a soccer game. Time for sharing a special family night at a restaurant, and time for family vacations. Skillful parents know they must share their lives in order to share their values. They know that it is while they are relaxing on the grass after fishing for a couple of hours that the special opportunity to communicate to an eleven-year-old might present itself. The effective dad does not miss the moment.

"Son, when I was about your age a struggle began in my life. It dawned on me that there were other beings on the planet besides boys. I felt powerful urges inside me and wondered if some of these beautiful creatures called girls would ever want me. Some of the guys at school stole peeks at *Playboy*. Others began to boast about their sexual prowess. I had to ask myself how I felt about sex and lust and how to deal with those powerful forces inside me. God's Word gave me the right answers. They helped me to know that I would enjoy sex in His time, according to His design, and they protected me from some serious mistakes. I want to pass His truth about sex on to you.''

Parents who invest the time necessary to develop intimacy with their children take the most powerful step toward inoculating them against immorality. Good sex education begins with parents who have taken time to genuinely know their kids.

Though my own dad was an itinerant evangelist and director of a large youth organization, I am thankful that he had time for me. I remember his cheering me on at midget league football games Saturday morning at 9:00 though he had a live, nationwide radio broadcast to do at 7:30 Saturday night. He was there in the spring of my eighth grade year when the opposing shortstop snagged three of my line drives, and we lost the baseball championship.

Mom was always there when I arrived home from school. I remember running up the stairs and into her bedroom. In spite of chronic health problems, she had time to chat about my day. She assured her husky ten-year-old that he would grow taller and thinner. Girls would become interested in him some day. My parents gave me more than preaching. They gave me themselves. Therefore I listened when Dad and Mom talked to me about the facts of life.

Relationship is the first priority. However, it is not enough. Our kids need right answers.

THE DIVINE ANSWERS

The parents in Proverbs give more than time to their children. They give inspired guidance. Observe how they refer to their teaching as "wisdom," "understanding," and "knowledge." They exhort their kids to memorize and internalize their instructions. They make the claim that if their children will listen, they will enjoy safe sex. How can these parents be so confident that they know the true moral standards? Is this not parental arrogance?

If I spoke that way of my own personal authority, it would be pretentious. But Proverbs does not present merely human values. God breathes through the proverbial wisdom. It is not ancient personal opinion but the design plan for skillful sexual living, and it comes straight from the divine Architect's drawing board.

These sexual standards have been inherent in the created order for thousands of years and for all cultures. If obeyed, they produce enjoyment. If broken, sexual life fractures. Just like the tablets of Moses and the revelation of the prophets, the wise man's counsel has the authority of the supreme Ruler of the universe. Proverbs' counsel is God's burning lamp, illuminating the path to healthy, fulfilling sexual relationships (cf. Proverbs 6:23; Psalm 119:105). In a society where the only absolute states that there are no absolutes, Proverbs challenges parents to decide whether their authority will be Dr. Ruth, Dr. Money, the latest poll in *Cosmopolitan*, or the enduring divine revelation recorded in the Scriptures.

In *The Closing of the American Mind* Dr. Allan Bloom argues against the modern dictum that "all things are relative" and challenges America to return to "fundamental principles" and to "moral virtues."* I contend that Proverbs is a fountainhead for this moral virtue. The wise sex teacher must begin with the proverbial fundamentals.

Without blush Proverbs introduces the young adolescent boy to two stunning women, Lady Wisdom and Lady Folly. Lady Wisdom personifies the ecstasy to be enjoyed by the young person who chooses to embrace morality and marital fidelity. Lady Folly personifies the electrifying thrill of lust but also the shocking, burned-out end of those who choose the animal aspect of sexual desire. These two women embody two choices, one of which will lead to success in sexual relationships and the other to disaster.

The parents in Proverbs seek to entice their children to fall in love with Lady Wisdom and to see through the seductive schemes of Lady Folly. Contemporary parents must be aware of these two women and know their characters thoroughly if they hope to be healthy sex teachers for their children. Let us begin by meeting Lady Folly. What does God want His children to know about a prostitute's boudoir?

*Allan Bloom, *The Closing of the American Mind* (New York: Simon & Schuster, 1987).

THINK ABOUT IT

1. Why is it difficult for us as parents to talk to our children about sexuality? Why is it necessary for us to come to terms with our own sexual urges in order to be able to talk wisely about this area with our children?

2. On the way to get a pizza or a Big Mac® with one of your teens ask him or her what health class is teaching about the biological facts of sex, the danger of venereal diseases, and the most effective preventions against infection. Don't be too quick to jump in and give your views concerning these matters. Ask questions and first discover what's going on inside your son or daughter in this area. "He who answers before listening—that is his folly and shame" (18:13).

3. Make a list of the dominant sources of information concerning sex in our culture. Evaluate the truthfulness of these sources.

4. Pray together as husband and wife that neither of you will be threatened by the young virility of your teens but will openly share biblical sex values with them.

10

The Seductress

Brad is fourteen. The fuzz above his upper lip has finally thickened into whiskers, and his husky 125 pounds are spread over a five-foot seven-inch frame instead of that cursed four-foot eleven-inch height he has been teased about for two years. He's been watching girls with admiration since he was eleven. When a pair of long, slender legs walk by, his eyes are easily captured. But none of these desirable creatures has ever noticed him. Barbara, a seventeen-year-old senior, changes all this.

She notices Brad his first day of high school. In fact, she takes him under her wing. She sits by him at lunch. Gives him a ride home from school and invites him to parties on the weekend. "Brad, I can't believe you're only a ninth-grader. You're so mature for your age. I've never been able to open up like this with a guy. My parents never have time to listen. How could I make it without you?"

Barbara does more than talk. During breaks between classes she holds his hand. At a movie she places her hand gently on his thigh. Dropping him off at his house after school, she kisses him strongly on the lips. One afternoon she drives past Brad's street and pulls into her own driveway. The garage is empty. Both her parents are away at work.

"Come on in for a few minutes," she invites.

Like a spark igniting gasoline, Brad's passion could become inflamed. To walk inside would mean giving something to a girl who actually cared little about him what he would never be able to give away for the first time again. What could Brad's parents teach him that would help him to say no at this crucial point in his life? How could they implant in his mind the discretion to enable him to see through Barbara's flattery in the early stages of the relationship? Our kids, like Brad, will probably face Barbara's invitation. How does God prepare His children for this encounter? What does God want our kids to know about seduction and its consequences?

Proverbs responds to the sexual potency of the young by talking frankly about immorality's con game. Proverbs challenges our kids to consider what has always been true about illicit pleasure. Its teaching method uses the art of storytelling to help children imagine seduction and its consequences before they actually face it in the hallways of their junior high or high school. Proverbs 7 presents one of wisdom's dramatic presentations.

The main characters, the naive victim and the cunning huntress, walk out onto the stage of life. The parent invites his sons to listen to seduction's smooth words, smell her enchanting perfume, and observe her stunning features. The teenager begins to feel the undertow of her proposition. Then at the moment of critical decision the skilled storyteller pulls the cloak of deception away and drives home the devastating consequences of falling prey to immorality's con.

Our young people daily experience this dramatic method of communicating values. The tragedy is that many movies, videos, and songs lie about the consequences of sex outside of marriage. The "party animal" becomes a hero surrounded by gorgeous women. Sitcoms assume teens who "go together" will soon go to bed together. Isolating your children will not silence these false messages. Authors and directors with strong ethical convictions need to combat this deception. We must reclaim the power of the story for good in training young men and women in our society, instead of exploiting their naivete for material gain. Parents need to replace the perverted messages from Prince, Madonna, and Motley Crüe with the valid ethics of explicit biblical narratives, such as those of Joseph and Potiphar's wife, Samson and Delilah, and David and Bathsheba. The Bible is hardly prudish about sex, but it is honest. Sons and daughters must hear about sex from God's perspective.

Solomon's sex education could be addressed only to the young men, for they would be the ones most likely to face the temptation of the street. Apparently, the daughters in the tenth century B.C. had the sense to know that sex for a woman involved much more than a few minutes of physical ecstasy. Also, the prevailing social custom of ancient Israel kept the girls at home under the loving care and protection of their fathers until the right husband could be found.

Today our daughters are exposed to the fast lanes of college life or the singles scene of a large city to the same degree as our sons. Consequently, our girls, as well as our boys, need to listen to the principles taught in Proverbs, for the "mysterious woman" of Proverbs 7 is far more than a literal woman of the street. She represents all the obsession and intrigue of illicit sex for both males and females.

The Victim

For at the window of my house
   I looked down through the lattice
and discerned among the naive a young man
   void of common sense and will.
Passing along the street near her corner
   in the evening twilight and as the dark of night set in
he took the steps which led to her house.

(7:6-9)

The entire book of Proverbs is an attempt to keep this young simpleton out of trouble. But as we learned in chapter 1, he is headstrong and cocky. He thinks he knows more than his instructors, and his arrogant naivete leads him to the wrong place at the right time. He knows where the woman lives. He knows the time of night she will be available, and he lacks the willpower to control the passion of his glands.

This is the teenager who has nothing to do on a Friday night except cruise the streets. His plan? Go out with the guys, look at the pretty girls. and boast about the one he will conquer. When Dad and Mom ask, "Where are you going tonight? What time will you be in?" he grunts and responds under his breath, "I don't know. I'm just going out with some of my friends.'' Adulthood to this young man means his dad and mom no longer have the right to know where he goes or what he does.

This unplanned "going out" is naive. If we allow it to occur, we are foolish. Mary is my effective ally in combating my male passivity when it comes to making our teenagers spell out their plans. Asking where they are, what they are doing, who they are with, and what time they will be in is not distrust. It is our responsibility of love. We must care enough to demand a plan. Places, activities, and times need to be nailed down so that love can make the right connections if problems arise. Life gets dangerous for kids when parents don't know where they are or who they are with, for a cat is on the prowl.

THE HUNTRESS

> Now a woman comes to meet him
>   dressed as a prostitute with hidden motives.
> She is boisterous and rebellious.
>   Her feet will not settle down in her house.
> First in the street, then in the open plazas,
>   finally near every corner she lurks to ambush.
>   (7:10-12)

The young man believes he is looking for love. The huntress knows she is hunting her game. The skillful sex teacher exposes the clothes and character of this female Don Juan.

DRESSED AS A PROSTITUTE

She is dressed to kill. Like the Venus's-flytrap, her gorgeous appearance is the captivating pull of death. This is no common street woman but a high-class number. Her carefully painted lips ooze an invitation to kiss (5:3). The flash of her eyes causes numbness to invade the young man's brain as the Novocain® of lust dulls his senses (6:25). The legitimate wife uses the sensuousness of her lips and eyes to arouse her husband to the joys of intimacy (Song of Songs 4:1, 11), but this immoral black widow uses these feminine charms to spin her web of death. She knows that the path to a man's body begins with an assault against his eyes.

HIDDEN MOTIVES

Sacred wedding vows mean nothing to the huntress. Years ago she screamed at her young husband and slammed the door of their home in his face. She abandoned this friend of her youth (2:17) to walk out into the night life. Now she hunts for the intoxication of sex with virgin men. These physical highs turn her life into the exhilaration of the present moment and obscure any concern regarding where her life might be going (4:6). Her boisterous defiance of domestic life mocks feminine gentleness and quietness (7:11). Her arrogant nonconformity causes other women to regard her with suspicion, but men find her fascinating and irresistible. They believe life with her would bring ultimate sex. Her soft skin blinds them to the granite hardness of her soul. Her words, however, (even more than her appearance) inject her most potent venom.

THE PROPOSITION

She seized him and kissed him.
   With an impudent face she said,
"I have prepared a sacrificial meal.
Today I fulfilled my vows.
So I came to meet you,
to look for you, and now I have finally found you.
My bed is made
   with the finest Egyptian linens.
I sprinkled it with exotic perfumes.
Come on! Let's drink our fill of sex until the morning.
   Let's enjoy love.
For the man is not at home;
   he is gone on a long trip.
He took plenty of money with him
   and won't return until the full moon."

(7:13-20)

The smooth tongue of the adulteress baits the young man with three lies: it's a holiday, a time for exceptions; it's your moment to become a man; and it's your opportunity to discover the pleasure of satin sheets and obsession.

THE TIME FOR EXCEPTIONS

In the ancient world the completion of a religious vow was commemorated by bringing a fellowship offering to the Temple. Part of this meat was offered to the deity as a burnt offering, some was given to the priest, and the rest was eaten by the offerer that day (Leviticus 7:11-15). Special holidays were opportune times for completing such vows. Thus the temptress informs the young man that a delicious steak waits to be eaten at her table. It is their night to celebrate. An evening to remember awaits him. Everyone knows that holidays are times for exceptions. Briefly forget the usual standards. Besides, this isn't some wicked street-walker but a good religious girl. After all, had she not been at the Temple offering sacrifices?

Our kids must be warned about the danger of the "special time," such as prom night, the night before a boyfriend or girlfriend leaves for college or reports for basic training, Mardi Gras in New Orleans, or Carnival in Rio. Immorality whispers during these times, "Ordinarily you would not do this, but this is a special moment." Our kids must also be informed that this lie can be heard not only after an acid rock concert but also after a church youth group social. Religious activity is no wall against the assault of lust.

I was sitting in a seminary classroom with twenty other men studying Ephesians 4. Being immersed in parsing Greek verbs and analyzing the grammar, most of us did not note the content of Paul's warning concerning the threat of sexual impurity. "Having lost all sensitivity, they have given themselves over to sensuality so as to indulge in every kind of impurity, with a continual lust for more" (Ephesians 4:19; NIV).

One of my classmates, however, was not deaf to Paul's concern that day. Allan was a husky, masculine fellow, but his shoulders began to shake. His eyes welled with tears. "Guys, I need you all to pray for my wife and me. She's eight months pregnant, and I'm afraid something will not be right with our baby. My fear is not just due to first-baby jitters. When I was fifteen, I went to Rio during Carnival, met a knockout Brazilian, and we had relations. Just a holiday fling, but a month after I returned home I felt lousy. A doctor checked me out and gave me the news I had contracted a venereal disease.

"Later when I met Judy and we got serious about marriage, I confessed my immorality and my past infection. She forgave me, and we went ahead with the wedding. Since she became pregnant, however, I am haunted with the fear that somehow my wife and baby could suffer because of my foolishness."

Our class put the Greek parsing on hold until the next period as we devoted the rest of the hour to praying for Judy and Allan. A month later the Lord graciously answered our prayers by giving them a healthy child.

Our heavenly Father is merciful. There was no need for Allan to fear. Penicillin had effectively cleansed his system, but his experience, even before the AIDS assault, warns us that a brief holiday fling can yield years of fear and pain. The holiday time must never become a time for making unethical exceptions.

The sequel to Allan's story warns against a more serious infection. Allan's struggle did not cease in Rio. The time for exceptions had infected him not only with a physical disease but also with a recurring moral weakness penicillin could never cure.

After graduation he became an associate pastor. I heard excellent reports concerning his effective ministry of working with singles in a large church. About two years into the ministry, however, the report was no longer filled with blessing. Allan had to leave his church because he had been unfaithful to Judy.

Warning! Immorality lurks when warm brother-sister relationships generated by Christ's love give way to sexual desires ignited by Satan.

THE TIME TO BE MACHO

The huntress's sacrificial meal attempts to reach the young man's heart through his stomach. But she is far too cunning not to recognize the most direct passage to a man's heart—through his pride. "I came to meet you, to look for you, and now I have finally found you" (7:15).

Like Brad at the beginning of this chapter, a fourteen-year-old might be physically grown and filled out, yet internally he can still feel like the ten-year-old the girls laughed at or treated like a little brother. In an attempt to compensate for this poor self-image, the naive teenager often puts on macho airs. He talks sex and flirts with the girls. Many of the girls are repulsed by his behavior at first, but he soon finds that some are more than willing to fulfill his fantasies. The huntress flatters this vulnerable pride and pushes the young man into a life of being consumed by the flames of lust.

Our sons must be warned about the smooth-tongued woman who flatters their pride, but our daughters must be warned about the "wounded puppy" who appeals to their instinct to care for the misunderstood and rejected. This is the young man who acts like the devil but confides to a beautiful young virgin that his heart is pure as gold underneath. She can redeem him. Her motherly instincts yearn to rescue this poor boy from all the misunderstanding and hurt. Before they encounter this seduction, our daughters must be taught that they will have plenty of opportunity to mother real children if God blesses them with a family. Husbands, on the other hand, are to be respected not mothered.

THE TIME FOR SATIN SHEETS AND OBSESSION

Adolescence should begin the process of learning to control the potential fire in your groin. Helping our teens to face sexual passion and control it, instead of ignoring its reality, is the parent's role. The father of Proverbs 7 explains how passion is aroused through the senses. Sexy sights, exotic smells, and sensuous touches rev a boy's sexual motor, and the huntress knows how to fire all the cylinders. Inside her apartment the stereo plays Ravel's *Boléro*. Her king-sized bed is turned down, and the scent of Fantasy® fills the air. She slips into something "more comfortable" and invites her young man to come and drink deeply of love. This is the scene described in Proverbs 7:16-18.

Immorality consistently confuses love with lust. Passion takes the place of commitment. As the hormones surge, faithfulness, purity, truthfulness, and self-control become forgotten concepts in the moment of explosive desire. Immorality always promises "We'll never get caught!" (7:19-20).

Richard was an executive for a Dallas computer firm. A pending contract necessitated a quick two-day trip to Los Angeles. His daughter, Deborah, was a sophomore at a large Southern California University. Arriving late, he was not able to give her a call, telling her he was there. While grabbing supper in the hotel restaurant, an attractive woman walked by and flipped a card on his table. When he returned to his room, he took the card from his shirt pocket.

"I've seen it on TV and in the movies. I've read about it in novels. What would it be like to have sex with another woman? Just this once! No one will ever know."

He dialed the number. In a few minutes he heard high heels clicking down the hall and then a knock on his door. Opening the door, he gasped.

Deborah stood before him.

Immorality consistently promises no one will ever find out. Gary Hart, John Tower, and Richard, that unknown executive in Dallas, never imagined that their private indiscretion would be laid bare. For centuries, the hard facts have proved that immorality has a tendency to come out of the shadows and accuse its victims in public. Dr. Bruce Waltke related the incident concerning his friend Richard while teaching a doctoral course on Proverbs. The last I heard, Richard was being blackmailed by his daughter, who was threatening to tell her mom about her father's attempted one-night stand. That husband, his marriage, and his family need healing. We should be warned against listening to the seductive whisper: "It's a time for exceptions. Prove your manhood. Experience exotic pleasure. You will never get caught!"

Barbara jumps out of her car and begins to walk toward the front door. She expects Brad to follow. He opens the passenger door and gets out.

"Barb, it's 3:45. I need to get home. I've got a piano lesson tonight, and my Mom will kill me if I don't get some practicing in."

The real reason Brad did not follow his girlfriend into the house? A red light had begun to flash in his head. "Danger! Beware of the time for exceptions, the time to be macho, and the time for obsession. You will get caught!''

During a late-night talk with Brad while camping out together, his dad had wondered if his son was really tuned in. The incident with Barbara proved he was.

11
Preventatives and Cures

Correct sexual standards, not condoms, are the best preventatives against sexually transmitted diseases. But physical disease is only one of immorality's potential consequences. Straight talk about all the pain—physical, emotional, and social—that sexual sin can bring is one step we must take toward helping the next generation establish healthy sexual values.

The wise instructors in Proverbs offer far more than prophylactics to their sons. They give them the truth about the pit of sexual immorality. Illicit sex sometimes gives the thrill of a lifetime, but it is like plugging yourself into a 220-volt socket—electrifying, yet deadly. We must sound the alarm. Our sons and daughters must be instructed and warned that immorality begins with an idea. Read and heed the "No Trespassing" signs. Never forget the deadly consequences. If you do fall, remember that the heavenly Father offers to forgive.

GUARD YOUR THOUGHTS

> More than anything you protect, guard your heart, for the wellsprings of life flow from it. (4:23)

My oldest brother-in-law, John, was on vacation in Kansas City when he felt a sharp pain rather like indigestion after dinner. However, as a physician, he knew it was not from too much rich food. A quick trip to the emergency room and an EKG revealed that at thirty-five John was experiencing his first major heart attack. Five years and three bypass surgeries later, his body could no longer take it, and his Savior called him home. Our family experienced first-hand the importance of a healthy heart and the deadliness of a sick one. The heart is the source of physical life, and all the current concern about cholesterol is an attempt to guard it from disease.

Proverbs' primary concern is not with our blood pump but with the source of our moral and spiritual life. The command to "guard your heart" is not a warning to watch your cholesterol. It is a plea to guard against wrong ideas, which will clog the arteries of the soul.

Deep within our personality, wrong thinking about sex leads to sick actions in sexual relationships. At the control center of our being, thoughts and feelings generate the decisions that lead to actions, and this is where the battle begins. This is where Proverbs wants to inject the truth. This is where we must be on guard.

Our desires to satisfy sexual drives are not wrong in themselves. They are normal. The evil stems from our false belief that these desires can best be fulfilled in ways contrary to God's design and with partners He does not intend us to have. The abominable lie that we can bring love and meaning into our lives by breaking God's moral laws is the beginning of sin (Genesis 3:6). We must teach our children to recognize and detest this deception.

For men, the first assault is against the eye. A seductive glance from a forbidden woman captures his gaze. In his mind he begins to covet the experience of having intercourse with such a beauty. For many men this enslaving seduction begins with the shameless, high-gloss image of a pornographic centerfold or the high-tech wizardry of the cinema, where bigger-than-life beauties willingly shed their clothes. We must not pretend these thoughts do not invade our minds. Instead, we must decide to say no to their alluring invitation. We must correctly label them as attempts to get us to break the tenth commandment. Coveting, or lusting after, what God does not intend us to possess, is breaking the final commandment (Exodus 20:17). It is the first disobedience in sexual sin.

When a parent finds the swimsuit issue of *Sports Illustrated* underneath his twelve-year-old son's mattress, it is not the time for embarrassment and anger. The magazine needs to be trashed but without condemnation. We need to talk to him about why men drool over these photographs each winter and about why he felt compelled to sneak a peek. Would his desire to look at a woman's nakedness be wrong if the woman undressing were his wife? Does he think one of these women who will take money to expose themselves to millions of men would make a dependable life partner? Could he trust her? Lust never takes the time to contemplate the truth. The truth can slash lust's grip on our minds.

Straightforward, honest discussions about sexual impulses —not denial—is necessary to protect our sons from being taken captive by the eyes of the seductress and from coveting her beauty in their hearts (6:25). Remember, it begins with an idea.

DANGER! NO TRESPASSING!

> Do not allow your heart to turn aside to her ways! Do not stray into her paths. (7:25)

> Keep far away from her, and do not go near the door to her house. (5:8)

There are places moral people do not go and paths they do not take. In the previous chapter we learned how the huntress seduces the naive adolescent because he is at the wrong place at the right time. His parents did not set boundaries, such as requiring explicit information about what he is doing, who he is with, and what reasonable time he will be home.

Moral kids do not create fake ID cards to go clubbing and buy drinks. They respect themselves enough to recognize that that kind of life belongs to drunkenness and immorality. Why give your virginity away to someone you hardly know while in a state too smashed to remember?

Wise teenaged couples respect the power of their sexual attraction and make a commitment not to be alone in homes or submit themselves to other situations where temptation could overwhelm them. We should discuss with our teen-agers the safeguards we exercise when, for example, we are away on a business trip, to maintain sexual purity. We need to discuss the kinds of doors open to them that could lead to immorality, and we can help them develop safeguards against these situations. All of us need to heed the "No Trespassing" signs.

Kids are tired of hearing adults preach about morality and proclaim, "Just say no," while watching these same adults say yes to the behaviors they warn against. Immorality is not an adolescent problem; it is a human problem, and all of us must follow the path that leads away from immorality's door. In our society it is a question of life and death.

THE DEADLY CONSEQUENCES

EXORBITANT PRICES

> Lest you give the bloom of your youth to others,
>   and your years to those who are mercilessly cruel,
> lest strangers grow fat on your productivity,
>   and your sweat enriches another's house.
>
> (5:9-10)

Free love is expensive. Though many teens have no concern for the future, we need to help our kids develop this awareness. Let's consider together the costs of immorality. If a couple in high school has relations and the girl becomes pregnant, who will pay the bill? Each day approximately half of the three thousand American teenaged girls who find themselves in this difficulty have an abortion. Should a helpless, developing infant be forced to pay the price for someone else's passion?

Suppose the couple decides to get married and keep the baby. How will they continue their education and cover the cost of the birth? What about the baby's care? How will the young husband deal with the resentment he may feel when his peers go away to college and he is left working menial jobs to keep food on the table for his premature family? How will the young mother feel at nineteen when her girl friends are going out on dates and she is left with a whining two-year-old not yet potty trained?

Suppose the boy will not assume responsibility for the child. Is it right for her parents to have to pay the expenses and, as is often the case, assume the responsibility? If her parents cannot afford it, the taxpayers pay the bill for welfare assistance. Teen couples have sex in the passion of the moment with their minds seared by the heat. Before they allow this passion to take over, they need to see the objective facts. When God's moral laws are broken, everyone in society pays.

Have we discussed with our sons what it means to "get caught with your pants down"? The extortion game is played like this: An attractive couple moves to town. The wife's provocative dress and beauty incite the men's imagination. Her husband is a workaholic. Obviously, he pays little attention to the romantic needs of his partner. She gets a job, and her co-workers notice her depression. She hungers for love. Her boss's son, home from college, works in the office with her, and soon they are sharing their lunch break. After one such lunch, she mentions, "I left Jack off at the airport this morning. His business will keep him away for more than a week. Why don't you come over to our place tonight and eat supper with me. I'm lonely and frightened in that big house."

The son arrives at her home and enjoys a good dinner. Her wine is exquisite, and she liberally provides refills. While watching TV, she puts her head on his shoulder. Her hand lightly touches his leg, and she kisses his neck. When his passions ignite, she pulls him to the floor.

Suddenly the darkened den blazes with light. With his pants down, the blinking young man faces her angry husband. "You are going to pay for this!" The naive young man never realizes that blackmail was the game all along. This game has been played for centuries, which explains why Proverbs warns against falling into the clutches of those who are merciless and cruel.

Have our children considered that if they do not control their sexual urges before marriage, a ceremony can hardly be expected to magically give them the gift of sexual control? Promiscuity in the teen years usually doesn't disappear in your twenties. After the vows, however, the sin is adultery, not fornication.

Marital unfaithfulness is a leading cause of divorce. The maligned party often hires a merciless lawyer. The adulterer's alimony payments will enrich another's house for many years (5:10). You can never pay enough to remove the disgrace (6:32-33) or buy forgiveness from those who are hurt (6:34-35).

Our children need to be taught from their youth that immorality demands exorbitant prices. The loss of wealth is the least of the concerns. Worse is the loss of health.

DEADLY DISEASES

> You will groan when your end comes,
>   when your body shrivels to skin and bones.
> Then you will say, "Why did I hate discipline?
>   Why did my heart spurn correction?
> Why wouldn't I listen to my teachers' voice?
>   Why wouldn't I open my ears to them?"
>   (5:11-12)

Why? Why? Why? The wise teachers in Proverbs know that the dying victim of sexual immorality is perhaps the most effective sermon on the need to make an early commitment to sexual purity. The hard realities of venereal disease argue for monogamous marriages and purity in every generation, whether it be the insanity of the nineteenth-century syphilis victim as his brain cortex shrank slowly and relentlessly or the POW-like skeleton of the AIDS victim in the 1980s, his body covered with purplish sores and his lungs starving for oxygen but defenseless against pneumonia.

I have argued throughout this discussion that ignorance is not bliss. In some cases it could mean death. Our teenagers must know that the HIV virus is transmitted by contaminated blood in transfusions, by intravenous drug abuse, and by sexual contact with an infected member of either sex. AIDS is a heterosexual—not just homosexual—disease. Our children should not only learn these facts from a government pamphlet but at home. We, the parents, underestimate the influence we have on our children's lives. A health class at school cannot compete with the power of our input.

We must tell them that though 70 percent of the AIDS casualties are homosexual and bisexual men and 20 percent are intravenous drug users, 4.3 percent are heterosexuals whose only risk factor was that they had intimate sexual contact with an infected partner. Surgeon General Koop wrote out his most effective prescription: abstinence before marriage and sex within a monogamous marriage. I would argue that condoms are a poor, uncertain alternative for those who refuse to commit themselves to purity; they are better than no protection yet hardly foolproof. Their effectiveness against AIDS isn't any better than their effectiveness as a birth control method, and married couples can attest to many unexpected pregnancies in spite of using the condom preventative.

Our children should have the same fear of immorality they would have of an archer poised to drill their gut with a hunting arrow (7:23). When tempted to indulge my illicit sexual appetites, I find the thought of an arrow protruding from my liver an effective deterrent.

As in Russian roulette, some play the game and apparently escape the consequences. The immoral individual fails to remember, however, that his or her private indiscretions could become public scandal any day.

RUINED REPUTATIONS

> I have come to the brink of complete ruin in the midst of the public hearings of the society. (5:14)

Whether indecent exposure occurs on Capitol Hill with Wayne Hayes or in the pulpit of Jimmy Swaggart, sexual sin costs you your reputation. Our society plays a dirty game. Novels, movies, and television communicate the image that everyone sleeps around at times. James Bond and even the eighties version of Superman fight never-ending battles against evil and injustice; but going to bed with beautiful women outside of marriage is not considered to be part of the evil. Yet when the decision comes to trust an individual with real responsibility in our society, suddenly adultery, liaisons with prostitutes, and even having been forced to get married in your youth becomes a blot against your character. If a person commits treason in his marriage, how can our nation be secure in his hands?

Gary Hart considers himself a victim of the media exposure and the prudery of the eighties. But even if he deliberately ignored Proverbs' exhortations, he could have read the identical advice in the writings of Ani, an Egyptian wise man who wrote to men aspiring for government positions.

Be on your guard against a woman from abroad, whom no one knows in her city. Do not gaze at her when she goes past, and do not know her carnally. She is deep water, the extent of which no one knows. A woman whose husband is far away, says daily to you "I am polished [pretty]!" when she has no witnesses. She waits and sets her trap. A great crime—and death, when it is known.*

The Star Wars generation may think they can change the rules. Yet for thousands of years, Donna Rices have ruined careers. Wise parents expose the nakedness of the media hype and teach their children moral standards that will make them credible candidates in every generation.

FORGIVENESS FOR THE FALLEN

Proverbs trains our children in the school of skillful living. Moral purity is the standard that protects them from ruined wealth, health, and reputation. This principle is life-saving, but what about those already drowning in immorality? Is there hope for the fallen?

Our children should learn the facts of sin in our homes, but they should also experience the warmth of forgiveness. James, a New Testament teacher in the tradition of Proverbs, unmasked immorality as the greedy passion for selfish pleasure (James 4:3-4). All sin is "adultery" against God and makes Him an enemy far more dangerous than a maligned partner in a marital suit. Yet He is not a merciless, cruel enemy. He offers grace to those who humbly admit their treachery and return to nearness with Him (Proverbs 3:34; James 4:6-8). Those who genuinely grieve over the personal hurt they have brought God and others experience God's gentle hands lifting them up to renewed purity. Jesus, the faithful Son, took the punishment. There is nothing left but to admit sin and ask our heavenly Daddy to forgive us. He never fails to restore His children to intimacy (1 John 1:9).

Satan's most cunning lie about sexual sin is that it is unforgivable. The words from the victim sound pious: "My case is hope-

*Walter Beyerlin, *Near Eastern Religious Texts Relating to the Old Testament* (Philadelphia: Westminster, 1978), p. 48.

less. The dirt is too ingrained for even God to clean." But this is a lie, a deception to be resisted (James 4:7). This is not humility but an arrogant refusal to accept God's truth about restoration. Hopelessness becomes the excuse for continued addiction to immorality. "God mocks the proud, but gives gracious forgiveness to the humble" (Proverbs 3:34; James 4:10).

Mick, a young Christian truck driver barreled his eighteen-wheeler down the night highway. Adultery had taken him captive during the past weeks. The lust for exotic sexual thrill, titillated by the raw pornography at truckstops, had driven him out of an eight-year marriage into a drunken, drug-filled world of illicit sex. Sessions with a Christian counselor could not penetrate the haze of immoral deceit. His believing wife slept alone while he gave his lust to a whore.

That night the eighteen-wheeler's cassette player cried out into the fog, "Are you living in an old man's rubble? Are you listening to the father of lies? If you are, then you're headed for trouble. If you listen too long you'll eventually die." The powerful words of Amy Grant's music rebuked Mick's heart. Where a counselor's verbal communication could not reach, the Holy Spirit's music pierced evil's armament. Mick began to return to faithfulness and purity.

Today, after much prayer and counsel, Mick is one with his Lord and with his wife. He is a believer in the proverbial preventatives, and he teaches these safeguards to his daughter. Use God's preventatives, and remember there is forgiveness and restoration for the guilty. "If we confess our sins, he is faithful and just and will forgive us our sins and purify us from all unrighteousness" (1 John 1:9; NIV).

12
The Intoxicating Wife

Gary and Susan settled into their seats and fastened their safety belts. The pace of the frantic day—pictures at 12:30, the wedding ceremony at 2:00, reception line from 2:45–3:30, the dash to the best man's car, the honking procession to the Austin airport, checking baggage, boarding the jet—finally eased. The newlyweds could settle back for three hours and try to relax.

"This is the best airline steak I have ever had. Even this artificial cake tastes like Mom's, fresh out of the oven." Gary tried to make small talk with Susan. His stomach remembered he had not eaten since the rehearsal dinner the night before. He watched Susan struggle to keep her eyes open as exhaustion rocked her to sleep. *I can't believe it! Our marriage is only two hours old, and already I've put my wife to sleep.* As Gary finished his tray, the thought of going to bed dominated his thoughts, and sleep was the last thing he wanted.

The mountains blocked the sun in the west, shooting spectacular reds, oranges, and yellows into the sunset as their flight circled Denver's airport. It seemed to take forever to reclaim their luggage but only moments to claim a brand-new rental car. They drove an hour west into the privacy of the mountains.

The lodge was nestled among the Aspens. In December, skiers would crowd to grab a room this close to the slopes. Yet in early June, only a few vacationers were in the lobby as the newlyweds registered and retired to their room.

"Gary, go ahead and use the bathroom first, I'll unpack our things." Susan tried to quiet her nerves by placing their clothes in the drawers. In less than two minutes Gary's teeth were brushed, and he made his reentry into their room dressed in the brand-new, white, silk pajamas his mom had commanded him to wear.

"Your turn, honey."

It doesn't take a man long to take care of things before he goes to bed, Susan thought as she disappeared into the bathroom with a small suitcase. Gary waited.

Alone in the bathroom, Susan was petrified. Since puberty her dad had warned her about immorality. When her friends in high school boasted of their prowess in bed, she braced herself against the peer pressure and guarded her virginity. When she and Gary began going together, they carefully controlled the physical side of their relationship. Susan appreciated Gary's patience, and his self-control won her trust. Both decided to save intercourse for their wedding night. The night was now here.

Susan loved Gary. She knew the biological mechanics of intercourse, but as her satin skin became rough with goose bumps, the wedding night jitters became dark fears.

Susan's parents had done an excellent job of warning her against the pit of sexual immorality, but they had not spoken freely to her about the fountain of marital, sexual love. They, like many parents, believed that telling teenagers too much about the joys of sex in marriage would entice them to eat the fruit too soon. The result: Susan knew in her mind that God smiled upon sex in marriage, but her emotions still screamed, "It's dirty and ugly!" How can we warn our kids against the deadly consequences of immorality without causing their emotions to become frigid?

We have listened as the parents in Proverbs warn against the deadly consequences of sexual sin. Christian teens constantly hear these words of warning. Do we share with them equally about the positive side of sex? Proverbs 5:15-23 stops sounding the dreadful alarms and goes on to ring the bells of celebration. The Creator wants His kids to relish the intoxicating pleasure of making love in marriage. The Bible is pure but never prudish about sex.

THE EXCLUSIVE FOUNTAIN

Drink water from your own cistern,
    flowing water from your own well.
Why should your springs overflow in the street,
    channels of water in the public squares?
Let them be for yourself alone,
    never shared with strangers.
Let your fountain be blessed,
    and rejoice in the wife of your youth.
    (5:15-17)

In a culture where an ice cold drink is just a refrigerator away, with the choice of cubed or crushed ice, the priceless prize of a private garden fountain is not appreciated. In the arid regions of ancient Palestine, men killed for exclusive rights to a well. The wise Israelite father compared this cherished pleasure of a drink to the refreshing pleasures of monogamous sex. We could paraphrase his thought this way: "Son, making love in marriage is the coolness of Rocky Mountain spring water on parched lips when the temperature soars above 100 degrees. Drink only from your private, unpolluted source!" (cf. Song of Solomon 4:15).

After commending sexual refreshment in marriage, the father contrasts the ugliness of taking this exclusive pleasure and making it cheap by having sex with multiple partners. Sex is too exquisite to share with someone you happen to meet at a party or on the street. The father in Proverbs compares casual sex to the wastefulness of throwing sparkling springwater into the gutter. The threat of AIDS sends a similar cold chill through our modern swinging singles scene.

Observe the dirty graffiti used for sex in the marketplace, and you will see how the purity of sex becomes more filthy than slush on a New York City street in winter when open lust replaces exclusive devotion.

God's special gift issuing from the pleasures of marital love are the children conceived in this union (5:18; cf. Psalm 127:3-5). Immorality breeds homeless, uncared-for street orphans (5:16). Exclusive marital intercourse gives birth to cherished kids with a dad and mom to help them learn to live. From the Asian-American castaways in the streets of Saigon to the corpses of aborted babies at U.S. clinics, immorality is always the enemy of children.

THE EXHILARATING PLEASURE

Rejoice in the wife of your youth!
A lovely doe, a graceful deer—
    be intoxicated with her breasts always,
    be drunk continually with her sensuous love-making.
Why go astray and get drunk sexually with a stranger?
    Why would you ever embrace the chest of a treacher-
    ous immoral woman?

                                                                (5:18-20)

Obviously this father knows the intense, satisfying high of intercourse with the one woman who has promised to make love only with him. He teaches his son the truth about where the lasting sexual highs can be found. This father shares the romantic secret of using caressing words before caressing with his hands in love. Not uptight about talking about sex with his son, the poet in him expresses himself. He compares a young wife's physical grace and beauty to the gentle sensuousness of a young doe.

Without turning red he speaks to his son about the intoxication a wife's body can bring her husband. If the stuffy Victorian objects to speaking with teenagers about the sexual thrill a woman's body can bring in a marriage, he or she should know that the original Hebrew text is more erotically explicit than I have been in my translation.

In chapter 14 we will devote an entire chapter to warnings about alcoholic intoxication, but here let us examine how sexual intoxication with your wife is a divine imperative (cf. 1 Corinthians 7:2-5). The intense ecstasy of marital intercourse is the only divinely applauded inebriation I know of in Scripture. When it comes to frank discussions with our young people about the thrills of sex in marriage, our prudishness will not keep them from discovering the details of intercourse. It simply guarantees that they often learn these facts from the serpent's sources—locker rooms, novels, movies, and supposedly "amoral" discussions in health class. This perpetuates Satan's lie that God is the Scrooge of sexual pleasure.

"Love God and become celibate, or reject Him and fulfill your sexual dreams." Godly parents attack this lie with the truth about sex from Proverbs. We should read and discuss Song of Solomon, God's celebration of marital intercourse, with our teenagers. We must resist the Christian culture's history of asceticism toward sex. If we believe in the authority of the Bible above religious prudery, we should not be afraid to expose our children to God's thoughts in His Word concerning the erotic intoxication of marital sex.

THE SACRED MEANING

For this reason a man will leave his father and mother and be joined to his wife, and the two will become one flesh. (Genesis 2:24)

This is a profound mystery—but I am talking about Christ and the church. (Ephesians 5:31-32)

God would hardly take something dirty and ugly and use it as His artistic masterpiece to depict physically the intense intimacy and devotion enjoyed by Christ and His bride. Priceless works of art are honored in guarded, exclusive museums; they are not passed around on the street. The sacredness of sex as an object lesson in the oneness believers enjoy with Christ must be guarded in the hallowed halls of marriage. This explains God's hatred of promiscuity and His satisfaction in seeing His children make love in marriage. The author of Hebrews summarized the Heavenly Father's sexual views: "Marriage is to be prized and honored always, and marital intercourse considered pure. The value God places on marital love explains why He judges fornicators and adulterers" (Hebrews 13:4).

Susan does not need to despair because of her goose bumps as she faces a new experience. She can be certain she is doing nothing wrong. Her heavenly Dad will be pleased when she joins with her husband. Gary and Susan do not need to be embarrassed by their fumbling attempts as they begin to learn the art of love. They have a lifetime to learn how to drink deeply of the pleasures. If, in the depths of their personalities, they grow confident that God smiles upon their physical union, they will discover their private, exclusive style for celebrating oneness in reflection of the unity they enjoy with their Savior. This is not cold theology but the reason marital sexuality is such a celebration in heaven and on earth. "And they were both naked, the man and his wife, and they were unashamed" (Genesis 2:25).

13

God's Liberated Woman

Something rare and beautiful is deemed priceless. In our liberated society you can find effective women executives, doctors, lawyers, astronauts, judges, and politicians. A few years ago, finding women in such professions was rare, but if you interviewed women on college campuses across the United States today regarding their career choices, you would recognize that these kinds of achievements for women will probably cease to be the exception.

Mention the "biblical view of women" to some career-minded feminists and they picture silent slaves, barefoot and pregnant, locked inside their houses, forced to meet the needs of overbearing, chauvinistic husbands. They react to this traditional view with enthusiastic cheers for the woman who escapes from the drudgery of dusting, vacuuming, and wiping runny noses to the power, money, and travel of a career. Their hero is the woman who never spoiled her figure by giving birth to a child. They forget to mention that she spends Mother's Day in a high-class club with a couple of other divorcees and no family.

The adversary's distortions of the Architect's designs amaze me. He always pushes things to extremes, causing us to miss the Creator's intent. Proverbs attacks both male chauvinism and radical feminism. It does not call for women to be locked in their homes, covered from head to toe as in Islamic fundamentalism; neither does it view them as Venus's-flytraps, agents of seduction and death to be avoided.

What qualities does our heavenly Father cherish in a woman? These are the fashions our daughters need to allow God to develop in their lives. These are the qualities our sons need to look for in a lifelong ally. A competent, godly wife was rare three thousand years ago. Solomon could not find one, though he tried a thousand (Ecclesiastes 7:28), which says more about his character than about women in general. Such a woman is still rare today. When found, this gem is far more than an intoxicating playmate in bed. She is a priceless gift from the Lord—the personification of wisdom herself. "A home and wealth can be inherited from fathers or grandfathers, but a wife who acts with reason, forethought and self-control is a gift received only from the Lord" (19:14).

CONFIDENT TRUST

Who can find a noble wife?
    Her value far exceeds the cost of diamonds!
Her husband trusts her deeply in his heart,
    and he never lacks valuables.
She does him good, not harm,
    all the days of her life.

(31:10-12)

The designation "noble wife" should forever silence the charge of chauvinism against the Bible. Women are hardly to be treated as inferior, weak, and second-class. The phrase used to describe the wife of Proverbs 31 literally means "a woman of strength, might, and power." The same phrase describes King David's mighty warriors (2 Samuel 23:20; 24:2) and God's prowess against His enemies (Psalm 59:11). The gutsy widow, Ruth, who chose to leave her homeland and carve out an existence with her aged mother-in-law in a foreign land, was referred to as a "noble woman" by Boaz, the man who made her his wife and the grandmother of King David (Ruth 3:11). This coveted title describes a woman admired by all for her industry, discipline, and moral fiber. Dependability is the heart of her durable nobility.

Unlike the seductress, this woman remains faithful to her sacred marriage vows (2:16-17). She imitates her God by keeping her promises. She does not enter marriage for experimental purposes but for keeps. "Till death do us part" is not an anachronism in her ceremony. Consequently, her husband never doubts her commitment to him. Truthfulness is at the core of her personality, and a woman of integrity never plays around behind her husband. As Joseph communicated to Potiphar's wife, our sons and daughters need to view infidelity as a treasonous breech of trust and a relationship to be feared. But a son can trust his life to a valiant wife of integrity.

After twenty years of marriage, I admire Mary's truthful dependability more than ever. When we started dating in the summer of 1968 I knew immediately that this woman told it like it was; her lips were connected to her heart.

We had dated a couple of weeks near the end of the camping season. On our day off I invited her to a family picnic. After lunch we were sitting on a rock alone in the middle of an Adirondack mountain stream. "Dave," Mary turned away from the small talk, "is this only a summer romance for you, or does it mean something more? My heart is beginning to respond. If you're just having a good time at the end of camp, I want to know."

Mary's frank integrity forced me to come to grips with my own feelings. The next spring I asked her to marry me and gave her a diamond. We have now enjoyed twenty summers together as husband and wife, and I still treasure her straightforward honesty; trust is the foundation of a marriage.

When someone tells the truth, you can put your confidence in him or her. The wise father and mother of Proverbs warn us to never trust in money (11:28) or in self-sufficiency (28:26). Repeatedly, they exhort us instead to "trust in the Lord with all of our heart" (3:5; 16:20; 28:25; 29:25). When a man leans on the Lord and the Lord gives him the gift of a godly wife, Proverbs urges him to put confidence in her and in her abilities (31:11).

Biblical leadership never browbeats others into submission. It creates an environment of support and encouragement, so that others blossom into all that God desires them to be. His wife's talents do not intimidate the godly husband. When he discovers her special skills, he builds her confidence and praises her effectiveness. As a result he enjoys the dividends from this investment in her competence.

COMPETENT HOUSEHOLD MANAGEMENT

THE APPAREL MART

> She carefully searches for the right raw materials—
>   wool and flax,
> and then creatively works with her hands with plea-
>   sure. . . .
> She holds the wool or flax distaff in her hand,
>   and her fingers grasp the spindle. . . .
> When snow falls she is not worried about her family,
>   they are all clothed in warm scarlet wool. . . .
> For her beds she makes beautiful spreads.
> Her garments are fashioned in fine Egyptian linen
>   and Tyrian purple.
>
> (31:13, 19, 21-22)

Thumbing through McCalls®, Butterick®, and Simplicity® pattern books, pawing through piles of material, finding the right thread and buttons—this was a foreign world to me before marriage. No longer! Mary's sewing ability was hardly on my list of qualifications for a wife, but her expert skills put sport jackets on my back in seminary and clothes on her children when our household grew. In bachelorhood, clothes were not on my priority list, but now I realize they are a strategic necessity. Mary's sharp eye for sales can also dress her household in style.

Proverbs 31 portrays the noble wife as an astute buyer of material (v. 13), a creative designer (v. 13), a dexterous spinner of the thread (v. 19), and an expert tailor (v. 21). Before anyone demeans these tasks as "women's work," remember textiles, fashion design, manufacturing, and the marketing of apparel are big business. Manhattan reserves an entire district for garments. My brother-in-law earns a good living as an expert in the field of clothing. He would resent anyone's demeaning its importance.

Household furnishing was another one of those areas that hardly affected my life as a single. Who cared what was thrown over my blankets and sheets, or what material was hung around a window? Marriage opened my eyes to a miracle—even a cheap apartment could be transformed into a home by the touch of a skillful wife. Curtains and quilts can incredibly change decor.

When Mary asked Nonnie Lewis in our church to teach her to quilt, I did not realize this would transform the simple task of getting into bed at night into a tactical nightmare. The only place we had room to set up the quilting frame was directly above our bed. Each night she instructed me how to help her move the contraption up against the wall. Each night I questioned the worth of the sewing clique's spending hours talking and doing handwork on a spread-cover. A trip to Lancaster County, Pennsylvania, changed my mind.

Lancaster is the capital city of quilting, and as Mary took me from one store to the next she inquired about every new design and material combination. I asked about the prices. When we returned home, I approached Mary with an idea. "Honey, we have quilts on our beds, by our stove, and in the closet. Let's sell some of them. They're a gold mine." She did not respond favorably, but I have never again demeaned the expertise involved in sewing little scraps of material together in intricate patterns to make a work of art that is also practical. Our heavenly Dad is concerned not only about the quilts on our beds but also about the threads on our backs.

God's daughters should dress for Him. This does not mean that they should wear gunnysacks and combat boots. He does get furious when His daughters forget the needs of the poor and live only for extravagant clothes, jewelry, and perfume (Isaiah 3:16-24). But He also encourages a woman to enhance her beauty with tasteful dress. The poverty of His Son meant He had few clothes, but His garment at Calvary was so exquisite the Roman soldiers would not tear it (John 19:23-24). The noble wife wore dresses made of the finest materials. We are responsible to help our daughters be modest, not dowdy.

A little girl asked her grandmother, "Could you show me how to sew like you?" A young wife went to an elderly Texas woman and asked, "Could you teach me to quilt?" I thank the Lord that these skills were passed on from the last generation to my wife. I do not resent expert female surgeons, lawyers, or bank presidents. Yet they do concern me. In a society of day-care centers, career worries, and mortgage payments, who will have time to teach the household arts to the next generation of little girls?

THE CULINARY SPECIALIST

> She can be compared to the shrewd merchant with ships
> laden with valuable goods;
> she brings her groceries from a distance.
> She gets up before dawn
> and begins to prepare meals for her family
> and assign the duties of her household attendants.
>
> (31:14-15)

When I go to the grocery store for an item, I pick the one nearest to me, rush through the express line, and head for home. Mary searches the newspaper for coupons, reaches to the back of the shelf for the cans stamped with cheaper prices, and drives from one store to the next to catch all the bargains. The Phoenician merchants were the cunning buyers of the ancient world. The shrewd purchasing skills of a diligent American housewife would have given them stiff competition.

Food is another basic necessity. The wife who saves on the grocery bill and still feeds her family in style deserves all the praise we can give. The profession of housewife is not for couch potatoes (31:15, 18, 27). Before dawn she must hit the floor running to get lunches prepared and send the children to school. In the evening she must still have the energy to pat backs and sing softly as her children fade into sleep.

God's plan for our daughters may not include a husband and children. He has special responsibilities for singles. But all of our daughters and sons need to be raised to stand up and cheer for moms on Mother's Day. Effective management in a boardroom is nice, but effective management in a household is vital to all of our security.

COMPETENT BUSINESS EXPERTISE

TEXTILES

> She makes lightweight linen garments, and sells them. She also
> wholesales fine sashes to the Phoenician traders. (31:24)

We have already admired her family's attire. Her weaving and sewing skills do not end, however, with clothing her family. She converts her talents into profits. She persists in bartering with the wily traders of her day, and, as a result, the profits for her textile and clothing businesses are so strong that she decides to enter the real estate market.

REAL ESTATE AND VITICULTURE

> After careful consideration of a field, she buys it.
> From the profit of her sewing enterprises she plants a
>   vineyard.
> She hikes up her dress and gets down to business.
> She tastes the sweetness of harvest.
> Urged on by success she works late into the night.
> (31:16-18)

Hardly the cowed housewife, this woman confidently evaluates the real estate market and uncovers an investment opportunity. With her textile and clothing profits she invests in a field. After the transaction, she executes her plan and develops a vineyard, a major source of revenue in ancient Israel. Her daily workouts provide the physical strength she needs to cultivate and plant her vines (31:17, 25). Her confidence grows with each successful marketing of her crop. This hardly fits the traditional caricature of the biblical housewife, too afraid to sign her own checks or venture out into public. The wise husband will learn not to be insecure about his wife's successes.

Catherine's son and daughter were entering high school, and the family budget was squeezed. A few dollars for college could certainly help. An opportunity at a local real estate agency presented itself. A devoted housewife, Catherine debated going out into the business world. "My days of changing diapers and watching 'Sesame Street' with toddlers has slipped past," she reasoned. "John and Cathy are not helpless. If something comes up at school during the day—I'll make it clear from the beginning to my employers—I will leave, no matter what, and tend to my kids." Wondering if anyone would hire a woman with these priorities and stipulations, she interviewed for the job.

Catherine did more than get the position—she won major sales awards. She had a special knack for discerning the buyer's needs and fitting houses with these desires. She did leave the office when her teenagers needed her during the day and came home when they got out of school. When her nest emptied, the adjustment was easier. Already she and her husband had begun to move to a new page of their lives. They now had enough money in the bank to take some of those trips they had dreamed about.

A young mother of four children who are all under the age of seven must not read Proverbs 31 as a list of her day's required activities. After reading the above example about Catherine, she should not decide to go out and sell houses. She needs to read this section of Proverbs as an ideal sketch of a lifetime—a video documenting years, not a snapshot of a moment. Remember, the Proverbs 31 woman has adult children with families of their own (31:28). Our daughters must recognize that there is a time for everything; no need to cram a lifetime into a day. Let's help them think through the progressive stages of life and enjoy the unique opportunities at every step. This will protect them from Wonder Woman burnout.

GODLY INSTRUCTION AND MODELING

With an open hand she gets involved and aids those
  bowed down in affliction.
She reaches with both hands to those needing
  help. . . .
When she opens her mouth, she speaks wisdom.
Her tongue forms kind, dependable instruction.
(31:20, 26)

Though not a self-indulgent yuppie, this woman does have upward mobility. However, her eyes see past her own selfishness to the crying needs of the suffering. Those in the hospital can count on her visit. Those wiping away tears of grief can count on her for a warm meal. She never forgets to send peanut butter that the missionary cannot purchase for his or her kids, remembering that Peter Pan is hard to find in the jungle. Some of my greatest encouragement to continue to follow Christ has come from the unexpected gifts of love that godly women extend. From the godly mom of

Proverbs 31 to Dorcas of Joppa in Acts 9, God always extols the unselfish woman who fills her days with acts of kindness and love toward others. Hollywood will not produce a sitcom about her, but Jesus will praise her before His throne.

Quietness, not silence, is a virtue in a woman. The movie *Yentyl* debated a woman's right to read the Torah and study theology. Proverbs presents a woman who not only learns Torah but also teaches others (31:26). Together with her husband she warns her children against the dangers of illicit wealth and sex (1:8ff.; 6:20 ff.). The teaching of King Lemuel's mother concerning immorality and alcoholism (31:3-4) and the need for social justice (31:5-9) was so powerful that God chose to include it in His inspired writings. This mother's instruction on drinking will provide the basis of our discussion in the next chapter.

The godly wife is submissive to her husband and works for his good (31:12, 23; cf. Ephesians 5:21-24), but she is not inferior. She banks on family, not self-enhancement. As life matures, what interest does her investment yield?

APPLAUSE FROM GOD, FAMILY, AND FRIENDS

Her sons get up and bless her;
   her husband joins them, and sings her praises,
"Many women have lived nobly,
   but you have excelled higher than all of them."
A charming personality is deceptive and breathtaking
   beauty a vapor,
   but the woman who reverences the Lord, she is to be
   praised!
Give her the fruit of her hands;
   in the gates of the city honor her for her accomplishments.

(31:28-31)

The message is ancient, but our sons still need to hear it. Like the writer of Proverbs, Charles Dickens astutely penetrated human nature. Young David Copperfields are forever blinded by the flighty charm and beauty of delicate Doras. They overlook their undependableness and dream of the ecstasy of making love to such a creature. Their eyes are too immature to see the competent, quiet beauty of the sisterly Agnes. Proverbs 31 counsels that the Agneses, not the Doras, make the best wives. The most important quality in any woman is her commitment to the foundation of a skillful life—a reverential relationship with God.

The 1290 score on her ˋSAT won Nanette a National Merit Scholarship and the right to go to the university of her choice with all expenses paid. The pre-med department of Baylor University opened its arms to this young woman with the brainpower to maintain better than a 3.9 grade point average for four years. While studying biology and chemistry at Baylor, Nanette met another pre-med student only one year ahead of her.

Bob was her match in studies, and, instead of competing, they decided to join forces. A few weeks after Nanette's graduation from Baylor they married, and she joined Bob in attending the University of Texas Medical School at Galveston. With Bob in his second year and Nanette in her first, they faced the difficult grind together.

Their mutual encouragement and support helped both to excel. During Nanette's second year they began to look forward to a lot more than their graduation from medical school. Their first child was due in November.

About four months before the delivery, Nanette was reading Philippians 2:3-4, "Do nothing out of selfish ambition or vain conceit, but in humility consider others better than yourselves. Each of you should look not only to your own interests, but also to the interests of others" (Philippians 2:3-4; NIV). The Holy Spirit challenged her to evaluate her personal reasons for wanting to be a doctor. *Approval by others or concern for others? Recognition or a desire to heal the sick? Money or ministry?* Bob gave Nanette the space to work through the decision herself.

After finishing her exams, she decided that the hectic frenzy of juggling classes, labs, and tests with diapers, bottles, and babysitters was not the Lord's will for her. Nanette dropped out of med school and committed herself to the full-time profession of being a wife and raising small children. Bob and Nanette now enjoy not one but two children—Kristen, a three-year-old, and James Robert, sixteen months and a flaming redhead.

When I called her on the phone I could hear both kids crying for Mommy. "Nanette, don't you think you should reconsider and return to your medical training?"

She laughed, "Dave, I've never regretted my decision. I have time to read my Bible and pray. I can give a sympathetic ear to friends who need to talk on the phone. I have time to give myself to needs at church. I can give myself to Bob and the kids. There is one thing I am tired of hearing—the reaction I get from the contemporary society, 'How could you ever give up a medical career to be only a housewife!'"

Now in her twenties, Nanette most likely will have time later to invest her talents in endeavors outside her home, but for now, in spite of society's ridicule, I know two small children who are glad Mom decided to stay home. I believe they will grow up to sing her praises. Our homes and churches need to be places where wives and mothers are adored, praised, and applauded.

Leadership Blueprints

Separate from intoxication, immorality, and injustice;
get involved and assert godly leadership in the community.

14

The Spiked Punch Bowl

Newly inaugurated President George Bush called the Washington celebration "democracy's big day." Brent Stephens, a freshman representative, agreed, but for that country-boy-turned-congressman the celebration lasted longer than inauguration day.

Still awed by his seat in the House of Representatives, he felt he must oblige the nonstop evening reception circuit. Though drained financially by his wife's need for designer dresses and emotionally by the war generated by John Tower's nomination for secretary of defense, Brent dressed for yet another Saturday gala.

The 8:00 P.M. classical concert at the Kennedy Center had satisfied his soul. At 10:00 his stomach urged him to satisfy his hunger. Across the ballroom his wife struggled to waltz with one of the portly Washington elites. Before rescuing her, Brent decided to sample the serving tables smothered in fine cuisine and the silver bunch bowls—two large contraptions with Greek goddesses spouting continuous streams of refreshment from their mouths.

"How do you know which bowl to drink from?" Brent was glad the senior senator from New York was also reconnoitering the table. Protocol was strategic in Washington, and he did not intend to prove himself an idiot in his first months on the job. "Son, it depends upon what you mean by drink. Since the Tower debacle, this bowl here is for young congressmen who aspire to higher office. This spiked one is for those without such aspirations."

The irony of this joke is that when John Tower came to Washington, few believed too much alcohol at a Washington party could cost a man his career. Such modern ignorance is inexcusable. Three thousand years ago King Lemuel's mother warned her son about the danger of mixing drinks with government service. Throughout history, wine, like women, has ruined political careers. Our children need to be warned about the drug that costs our society more than $117 billion a year "in everything from medical bills to lost workdays" and causes more deaths than AIDS, heroin, cocaine, marijuana, and crack combined, according to Loran Archer, deputy director of the National Institute on Alcohol Abuse and Alcoholism (*Time*, November 30, 1987).

CONTROLLED BY THE SPIRITS

MOM'S INSPIRED COUNSEL

> The words of King Lemuel, an inspired correction, which his mother taught him. What, my son, what can I say to prepare you for rule; the son I carried for nine months, the son I prayed for? (31:1-2).

Like the wise mother in Proverbs 4:3, Lemuel's mom knows how to express her tender affection for her son. She remembers how she cherished the developing baby in her womb. She reminds him often that he came as an answer to her prayers. How different from some mothers who shred their children's sense of value by talking about their conception as a bad accident. We are reminded again that effective parental instruction begins in the womb of intimacy. Lemuel's mom wrestled with the need to prepare him for his position of power, and God chose to inspire the straightforward advice she gave.

THE INTOXICATION-INJUSTICE CONNECTION

> Do not give away your virility to immoral women,
>   your career to those who destroy kings.
> It is not right for kings, Lemuel—
>   it is not right for kings to drink wine,
>   or for rulers to ask, "Where are the hard drinks?";

lest they drink and forget what is decreed by law
    and twist the court's decision against all the children of
    oppression. . . .
Open your mouth for those unable to speak for them-
    selves,
    and defend the rights of all those who are deprived.
Open your mouth; render a just decision;
    plead the cause of the poor and the needy.

                                                    (31:3-5, 8-9)

Intoxication, like immorality, perverts justice. Exposed candidates cry out against the "injustice" of evaluating their fitness for public office on the basis of their conduct in private life. The mother in Proverbs had the common sense to know which judges drank too much, slept around with women, or wouldn't muster the moral fortitude to stand up for a black or Hispanic unjustly accused of stealing by the big-business landlord in town. Drunkenness fuels social injustice against the poor in every age. Our society needs governmental officials who will refuse bribes and will judge impartially. The underprivileged should be able to count on fairness in a courtroom. Drink demolishes this confidence.

Common decency screams, "Drunk driving destroys the lives of more than 23,000 people a year. Where are the laws to stop this homicide?" Common sense discerns the sad reality—the congressman who habitually drives home from parties drunk cannot be relied upon to vote to stiffen penalties for DWIs (those driving while intoxicated).*

My associate pastor served on the jury in a DWI case. As they deliberated in closed session, the evidence of the case glaringly portrayed the guilt of the defendant. He would lose his license, which was the required penalty at the time. One of the jurists began to argue, "Wait a minute! How is this man going to get to work? How will he continue to live a normal life? Which one of you hasn't had

*Known in many states as DUI (driving under the influence).

too much to drink at times? Remember this could be your neck some day!'' My friend responded, ''You have missed the point of this trial. If the defendant is guilty of breaking the law, he should face the legal penalty for this crime. The issue is not how this would affect our lives if we were facing the same judgment.'' The license was never taken away. The case stalled on a hung jury. Intoxication perverts justice.

My wife's fifteen-year-old brother was murdered by a drunk driver on New Year's Eve in 1981. The driver who struck David down was driving without a license—he had lost it as a result of three previous convictions.

The Department of Justice estimated that in 1987 nearly 174,000 inmates guilty of rape, burglaries, and assaults drank heavily before committing their crimes (*Time,* November 30, 1987). Like King Lemuel, our children need to be raised with a clear message from parents concerning the intoxication-injustice connection.

THE ANESTHETIZING SEDATIVE

> Give hard drink to the person who is dying,
>   wine to someone experiencing the intense bitterness of
>   grief.
> Let him drink and forget his poverty
>   and become unconscious to his bitter misery.
>   (31:6-7)

Ethanol, the active ingredient in strong drink, effectively numbs self-consciousness. Like other tranquilizers, such as Valium® and Librium®, it influences the synapses between neurons, thus retarding neurological function. This includes the brain. Lemuel's mother did not understand the biochemistry of neurotransmitters or that their inhibition causes exhilaration, loss of social restraint, slurred speech, distorted sensory perception, drowsiness, and blackouts. But she did appreciate the sedating value of alcohol for those facing extreme pain or terminal illness. Much as an oncologist gives morphine to the dying cancer patient, she counseled Lemuel to give alcohol to those experiencing intense misery. The tragedy in our culture is that, unlike Valium and Librium, which demand a physician's prescription, we sell alcohol along with Coke®

and Dr. Pepper® everywhere from basketball games to convenience stores.

In contrast to other psychoactive drugs, ethanol does not target specific nerve cells. It penetrates cells at will, and when taken in large doses harms almost every organ of the body. Myocardial disease, high blood pressure, stomach ulcers, shrunken testicles, infertility, birth defects, mental retardation, immune system deficiencies, cancer, and cirrhosis of the liver are the slow, persistent death tolls of over-drinking.

When a football teammate says, "Let's go out after the game. My older brother drove to the next county and got us a pickup full of Coors," our sons need to see a mental picture of a jaundiced hospital patient with a malfunctioning liver worn out from processing gallons of booze, suffering chronic blackouts, dying ten to twelve years earlier than his or her expected lifespan. Our children need to know that the initiation to this condition begins with, "Have a drink and prove you're a man!" A visit to the alcohol rehabilitation center at a local hospital and some interviews with recovering alcoholics could be some of the most effective training we give our children concerning the booze cartel in the United States.

I still remember a lesson my dad taught me as a five-year-old on a New York subway. His Saturday youth rally had gone late as usual. It was about 11:30 P.M. when the doors electronically slid open and we boarded the subway. Immediately, the stench of alcohol hit me. On the floor was an empty wallet and an unconscious drunk. His suit was expensive but torn and soiled. Blood trickled from scrapes on his face. On the wall above his head was posted the latest beer ad, in which a knockout-blonde at the side of a bronzed muscle builder toasted ice cold mugs and proclaimed the slogan "Here's to life!" As Dad knelt down to try to help the man, he pointed to the ad and said, "David, that's what the world says. This is what it is."

Modern pharmacology can offer sedatives without some of the potential hazards of ethanol for moments of extreme crisis. Any mind-altering drug taken in massive doses becomes poison. Those responsible for the good of others cannot afford to be slowly poisoned. God's children, like King Lemuel, are royalty. It will demand all our wits to be the "salt and light" Jesus desires us to be in a decaying society.

Sobriety will·also save God's children from some of the rough effects of companions who regularly drink alcohol—brawls (20:1; 23:29), wasted resources (21:17), psychotic hallucinations (23:33-34), and confusion (23:34). While I was visiting a hospital recently, a doctor told me that more than 80 percent of the patients were there due to conditions caused and aggravated by alcoholism. It is our number-one drug problem and a close second to cardiac arrest as a leading cause of death in the U.S. Imagine hearing this newsflash from Dan Rather *every night:* "Six hundred die in air disaster!" More than that die every day, either directly or indirectly, because of alcohol.

It sparkles in the crystal goblet and goes down dry and smooth. The alcohol companies sell the illusion that it will transform you into a great athlete or a stunning "party animal." Proverbs tells the truth. In the end, it strikes like a rattlesnake. Its venom is more potent than a cobra's (23:31-32). How can we help our kids control this snake?

CONTROLLED BY THE SPIRIT

Do not get drunk on wine, which leads to wasteful destructive living. Instead allow the Holy Spirit to fill you. (Ephesians 5:18)

Prohibition demonstrated that legislation cannot adequately control the human being's craving for "spirits." External rules can never cage our intense desire to feel good, laugh with friends, and celebrate life. At the cocktail party alcohol creates a euphoria and a freedom to socialize. The bar becomes a place to share deeply and find support from friends. This is Satan's counterfeit for the Body of Christ. He substitutes a deadly drug for the Holy Spirit. We must not locate the evil in the chemical but in ourselves. We are committed to the lie that we can meet the needs of our hearts without allowing God to be in control.

The slanderer's deception continues as he turns our gatherings at church into boring lectures instead of Holy Spirit-controlled celebrations of forgiveness and family intimacy. When our children do not see us making music together and freely expressing our thanksgiving to God for the gift of His Son, they become prime candidates for the enemy's church—the club circuit. We should be living models of the superiority of Spirit control over alcohol control. As they mature, our children must make the choice between living a life controlled by the "spirits" of alcohol and living a life controlled by the Holy Spirit of God. Again, we return to the individual's responsibility to decide who will be sovereign at the core of his being.

> For you have spent enough time in the past doing what pagans choose to do—living in debauchery, lust, drunkenness, orgies, carousing and detestable idolatry. . . . The end of all things is near. Therefore be clear minded and self-controlled so that you can pray. Above all, love each other deeply, because love covers over a multitude of sins. (1 Peter 4:3, 7-8; NIV)

God's children are all aspiring for higher office. Let's beware of the spiked punch bowl.

THINK ABOUT IT

1. Do you know a recovering alcoholic? Why not have him or her over for dinner? After the meal have him sit down in the living room with your entire family and share his experience. Let the kids ask the questions after you get things going.

2. Jonathan, Joel, and I went to a Texas Ranger baseball game. All around us quarts of beer were being consumed. One of the fans spilled his all over Jonathan. Later, a fight broke out, and a force of security guards had to keep it from exploding into a riot. On the way home I asked the boys how they felt about all the drinks served at the ball park and the mixed messages concerning alcohol that were communicated. What are some situations your family has experienced with the problems of drunkenness? Listen to your children's feelings and thoughts about some of these.

15
Word Power

Tom Clancy's war saga *Clear and Present Danger* runs for 656 pages. Where do all those words in an author come from? We do not need to look far. The average American opens his mouth to talk approximately 700 times a day. This adds up to approximately 3500 words daily, which means we communicate the equivalent word sum of a Tom Clancy blockbuster every couple of months. Unfortunately, this pile of words does not guarantee that we can weave together a mass of intricate, technical details into a riveting tale of espionage and war. We may not all be Tom Clancys, making millions on military-political adventures, yet Proverbs wants each of us to become an expert on the power of words, their limitations, their source, and the characteristics of wise word usage.

More important than mastering a word processing package on a computer is the need for our children to master word processing in their minds, as well as the ability to speak clearly to others. Wise verbal skills are a must for leadership. Harnessing this powerful flow from our mouth is the distinguishing mark of wisdom.

"We all stumble in many ways. If anyone is never at fault in what he says, he is a perfect man, able to keep his whole body in check" (James 3:2; NIV).

THE POWER OF WORDS

LIFE AND DEATH

> Death and life—they are in the power of the tongue; those who
> cherish words will eat their fruit. (18:21)

Winston Churchill used words to resurrect his nation and the
Allies. Hitler used words to bring about national genocide and personal suicide. Like Smokey the Bear, who teaches our kids about
forest fires, we need to help them appreciate how words can be used
to bring warmth or waste. Because the wise individual realizes the
awesome power in a word, he falls in love with language, including
the precise meaning of words, their emotional impact, and the exact
timing of their delivery.

He recognizes that wise teaching revives others like a bubbling
fountain or a nourishing meal. Correct instructions can protect others from deadly errors (10:21; 13:14). Wise words combat the lethal
weapons of a false witness in a courtroom by shooting straight to the
truth (12:6; 25:18). Like Daniel's appeasing Nebuchadnezzar's anger, the wise person knows that honest, reasoned speech can save
lives (16:13-14; cf. Daniel 2).

TO BRUISE OR TO SOOTHE

> There is a person who speaks without thinking like thrusts from a
> sword, but the tongue of the wise brings healing. (12:18)

Reckless words pierce personalities like sword thrusts (12:18);
subversive words crush spirits (15:4); and slanderous words destroy
friendships (16:27-28). Wicked, godless words burn down not only
personal lives but entire cities (11:9, 11; 16:27). Only wise, truthful, gentle words can put out the fires. Words can bruise like Mike
Tyson's fists, but they can also soothe like a nurse's gentle hands.

Gracious, kind words can lift a crushed spirit up from the pit of
depression (16:24). The individual dying of thirst in a desert of difficulties comes back to life with unexpected good news (25:25). Remember the good news from Egypt: "Joseph is alive and well!" It

gave his aged father, Jacob, the gift of a few more years of life (Genesis 45:27).

Counsel from the heart of a friend is the perfume of a relationship (27:9). Even when it smells more like antiseptic than perfume, the straightforward, honest rebuke of a friend is far better than the unexpressed devotion of a secret admirer (27:5). Our true friends will risk the relationship to tell us the truth. This is the friend who sticks closer than a brother (18:24).

TO REWARD OR RUIN

A person who guards his mouth preserves his life, but the person whose mouth is constantly open, destroys himself. (13:3)

The calloused hands of a carpenter bring him his living by building houses. The disciplined, skilled tongue of an orator earns him his living by building lives. Effective speaking is the manual labor of a leader (12:14). Like the farmer who plows and plants, the communicator brings in his sustaining harvest with words (18:20). As a pastor, one of my major responsibilities is to communicate effectively the concepts in God's Word each Sunday morning. In a tangible sense, I put food on my family's table by the hard work of teaching with my mouth.

The private Christian high school I attended twenty-six years ago could not afford state of the art microscopes or hundreds of histology slides. As a chemistry major in college, it took me two years to catch up on the technical data. Though my high school failed to excel in math and science classes, it did give me a training that has turned out to be far more valuable.

In the spring every student memorized a speech from a well-known orator. One by one, before the entire student body, we had to ascend the steps to the platform, put our hands down at our sides, and deliver the declamation. The best in the freshmen-sophomore and junior-senior divisions competed for "top gun" declaimer. This declamation contest, along with debate and the recitation of "readings," helped me to get over the fidgets and to focus on eye contact, audience sensitivity, and the thrill of moving a group with words. I am grateful for teachers in high school who made me speak before an audience.

I am also thankful for a dad who called on me at random for a word of public testimony in his evangelistic meetings. One afternoon my dad drove our family up to Plattsburgh, New York, to do a weekly television show. Usually a special guest rode along with us.

"Dad, is your special guest meeting us up there?"

"No," he replied and kept his eyes on the road.

"Are you going to give a message yourself?"

"No."

"Then what are you going to do for half an hour?"

He looked at the three of us kids and said, "Interview you guys."

The cameras almost made me wet my pants, but every time I get up to publicly proclaim God's Word I am thankful for a dad who gave me the confidence to speak. Kids do not have to be put on TV to learn how to speak. There are children's Sunday school classes, AWANA clubs, daily vacation Bible schools, and a host of other opportunities for our kids to mature in public speaking. In Midlothian our teenagers are practicing a drama from Romans for the Sunday morning worship service. Teenagers cannot complain about boredom in the Sunday morning worship when church leaders allow them the freedom to take part in it.

Our kids need to learn early—words can enrich others and feed your family. But the wrong words at the right time can ruin your career, such as Jimmy the Greek's racial slur on public broadcasting did (13:3; 21:23). Words can reward, but they can also ruin.

THE LIMITATION OF WORDS

As Derek Kidner, the English commentator, has analyzed in his book *Proverbs*, the wise individual, unlike the sluggard, understands that words are no substitute for actions (14:23). They cannot alter the facts (26:23-28; 24:12; 28:24), and they cannot compel a correct response (17:10).

We exposed the sugar-coated glaze over the sales pitch of the con artist (chapter 6) and the incorrigibility of the impenetrable block (chapter 3). We parents are responsible for communicating these essentials before we send our kids into the world. But we must accept the limitations of our words.

Words cannot force them to accept our values. If we could compel our kids to respond, we would be brainwashing them, not teaching them. We would destroy their will, which makes it possible for our children to love God with all their hearts.

THE MARKS OF WISE SPEECH

Like the brand indicating the ownership of prize, registered stock, here are the identifying characteristics of words that indicate that this mouth belongs to a wise person:

1. They are honest and fair (12:22; 16:13; 24:23-26).
2. They are few, not many (10:19; 17:28).
3. They are humble, not boastful (27:2).
4. They are patient, not nagging or argumentative (17:14; 19:13-14; 25:24; 27:15-16; 29:9).
5. They are private and confidential, not gossipy or slanderous (17:9; 20:19; 25:9-10).
6. They are careful, not hasty (12:16; 15:1; 18:13; 25:15; 29:20).
7. They are apt, not untimely (15:23; 25:11, 20).

Where do these kinds of words come from? Like an EKG, our words reveal the health of our heart.

THE SOURCE OF WISE WORDS

> Wisdom is found on the lips of the discerning, but a rod is for the back of those who lack heart. (10:13)

The person with "heart," or the ability to discern between right and wrong and between wisdom and foolishness, speaks consistently with such moral character. The person without this core uses his mouth destructively and pays the consequences. In his commentary *Proverbs*, F. Delitzsch quotes a Talmudic proverb that captures the reality: "That which a wise man gains by a hint a fool only obtains by a club." To control our tongues we must go to their source—our hearts. When the tongue is connected with a heart committed to God and His wisdom, it speaks words of life, healing, and edification.

This heart listens carefully to instruction (19:20) and carefully weighs its words (15:28). Recognizing that when one sleeps with dogs he catches fleas, the wise heart does not choose fools (13:20), short fuses (19:20; 22:24-25), or boozers (23:20) as its companions. Jesus stressed this word-heart connection: "For out of the overflow of the heart the mouth speaks. The good man brings good things out of the good stored up in him, and the evil man brings evil things out of the evil stored up in him." (Matthew 12:34*b*-35; NIV).

The telephone rang the alarm at 9:45 P.M. "Dave, I think Don, Martha's husband, suddenly died this evening." Praying that this tragic news was only a rumor, I drove out to Joshua's second grade teacher's home in the country. The tears on the faces of her ten- and fourteen-year-olds immediately informed me that the news was not a rumor.

Joshua adored his teacher, and when a substitute took his class the next day and the principal tenderly informed the class that they needed to pray for their teacher and her family in their loss, Joshua took it hard. That evening he prayed for his teacher. "Dear Jesus, Mrs. Wetzig is in the Castle of Despair like Pilgrim. She needs Promise to come and rescue her." When he finished praying, he crossed his hands behind his head, looked up at the ceiling and said, "Daddy, it's a good thing we have a man like Jesus around. He's the only one who makes any sense." Joshua's words told me that he had paid attention to the video series on *The Pilgrim's Progress* at church, but more important, they revealed the condition of his heart.

Those words from John Bunyan's 1678 classic and from a second grader's 1989 insights were the comfort and strength I used to close the funeral service the next afternoon. Sometimes "word power" is discovered in the mouth of a child.

16
God and Power Politics

I was raised in fundamentalism before the days of Jerry Falwell and the Moral Majority. Voting was our American responsibility, but involvement in politics was demeaned along with other unsavory occupations, such as bartending, gambling, and prostitution. It was drilled into my thinking that "a committed Christian could never be elected to public office. The only way to win would be to lie and bribe."

On the other hand, we lamented the tearing of the moral fabric of our nation and blamed much of this wreckage on the government. So the vicious cycle maintained itself—government was a place for godless manipulators; therefore the godly did not get involved in this arena. This guaranteed that the arena was often left only to those who rejected biblical morality.

The advent of the "born again" era through Jimmy Carter and Ronald Reagan and the cry of the Moral Majority, "Back to our Judeo-Christian roots," made the former aversion to political involvement among fundamentalists and evangelicals seem as quaint as a black Amish buggy, even among ourselves. Pat Robertson, a prominent evangelist, went so far as to resign his ordination in order to run for president. But as we flex our newfound political muscles, let us allow the wisdom of Proverbs to teach us and our kids some political savvy. Its balance can protect us from worshiping the political system as "the savior" and from withdrawing from it as "the satan."

Righteousness does exalt any nation, and sin is a disgrace to any people (14:34). But what do "righteousness" and "sin" look like from the perspective of Proverbs? How does God interact with power politics?

THE ULTIMATE SOVEREIGN

Like the irrigation canals, a king's heart is in the hand of the Lord; he directs it wherever he pleases. (21:1)

Governments, like individuals, must respect the Architect. He is the Author of the destiny of individuals and nations. Nebuchadnezzar, Alexander the Great, Julius Caesar, Charlemagne, Napoleon, Hitler, and Stalin all used to strut their stuff, but the tyranny of their reigns grieved God's heart and earned His retribution; none escaped the plot line He is writing.

Nations can pray to Marduk, Horus, the "ground of being," or the "force," but all people live in the time and territory of the biblical God. Biblical faith should never use the human sword to force compliance with the Lord's sovereignty, but it must recognize the fact that all nations are "under God"; every individual will ultimately give an account to his Creator. Governments that recognize this objective reality and obey His moral precepts receive His favor and blessing. Those who reject Him are eventually crushed by their fantasy that God can be ignored.

The principles presented in Proverbs are never limited to a segment of the American population called "evangelicals" or "born-againers." They cannot be sealed up in religious services like ancient artifacts in a museum. Proverbs claims that the following are the correct operating principles of all governments—theocracies, monarchies, and democracies (8:15-16). These standards were in place before any human government was instituted (8:22-30). Let's sketch some of these universals that our kids need to breathe from infancy.

UNIVERSAL GOVERNING PRINCIPLES

JUSTICE IN THE COURT

Truth, not word manipulation, is to be the issue at stake in the courtroom. Judges are to honor those that speak what is right (16:13). Governments that tolerate courts in which the guilty are declared innocent and the innocent declared guilty will be cursed by their people (24:23-25). Perjury must not go unpunished (19:5), and money must not alter the outcome of a trial (22:22-23). Those who plunder the poor will themselves be plundered by the Lord (22:23).

These divine requirements for the judicial system are obvious. We do not have to spend much time in court with lawyers, judges, and juries before we realize the pressing need for the American judicial system to apply these standards. If the Lord leads our kids to law school, these ethical values, not BMWs and Wall Street stocks, need to be their driving concerns. It will take prayer and all the legal acumen they possess to flesh out God's norms in specific court cases.

JUSTICE AND COMPASSION IN THE MARKETPLACE

Harvard Business School graduates might argue that the bottom line is profits, not ethics, but God, the ultimate chairman of the board, disagrees. His counsel is not ethereal either.

The tongue-in-cheek humor "We pretend to work, and they pretend to pay us" explains the economic collapse of Communism in Eastern Europe. When I was visiting Poland, a new friend asked me over lunch, "Dave, did you know that Adam and Eve were Communists?"

"No," I replied and kept chewing the lean supply of sausage.

He grinned. "They had no clothes, one apple between them, and thought they were living in Paradise." A ruling party cannot snuff out physicians, engineers, and other intellectuals like insects and expect to build a robust economy. Lenin forgot a simple principle from Proverbs: a nation cannot prosper when competence goes unrewarded and incompetence is not viewed as a disgrace (14:35). Socialized capitalism sometimes forgets this principle as well.

The free market, however, faces the danger of forgetting the divine imperative to maintain honest weights and measures in sales (11:1). God does not like it when goods are not weighed correctly and when consumers are ripped off by greedy businessmen (16:11). Without God's principles, capitalism also forgets compassion for the poor.

We must never gloat over the disaster of others (17:5). God is the defender of those in need. When we graciously give to those too feeble to help themselves, we actually make a loan to God. We can count on His repayment; He is never a security risk (19:17). If we fail to respond to the cries of the poor, someday we ourselves will cry and not be answered (21:13). Every form of exploitation must be condemned (22:22-23).

Business persons who apply the proverbs will be protected from upper-class bigotry, which either fails to give to the needs of the poor—classifying all of them as "lazy couch potatoes"—or assuages its guilt for its extravagance by making liberal handouts. Proverbs encourages generosity to the disabled but never forgets human dignity. Every honest man who works hard to develop his talents from the Lord should be rewarded for his efforts.

PATIENCE BEFORE WAR

The government that recognizes the Lord's rightful sovereignty will not depend upon its arsenal for final security (21:30-31). Personally, I do not believe the Scripture counsels nations to beat their swords into plowshares before the davidic Messiah rules over the world in Jerusalem. Proverbs does stress patient diplomacy over hot-tempered retaliation (16:32). If mobilization must take place, the battle plan requires the skills of many advisers to insure victory (20:18; 24:5-6). Slipping half-heartedly into war without the commitment of the people guarantees the multiplied loss of life as well as failure.

COMPETENCY AND MORALITY
IN POLITICAL APPOINTMENTS

Skill, not a party spoil system, should determine political appointments (19:6). Government officials should move up the ladder of power because of their pure motives and ability to express themselves clearly and graciously, not because of their Machiavellian pragmatism (22:11; 25:15). As in the marketplace, competence should be recognized in the halls of state (19:10; 22:29). If all this sounds anachronistic and naive in the sophisticated world of Washington today, let me state that it is not the ancient principles that will bring the last laugh but the ruinous stupidity of modern relativism, which ignores biblical ethics.

The voice of wisdom will not be heard in the court, boardroom, or legislature if those committed to God and His instructions do not get involved.

INVOLVEMENT—
THE RESPONSIBILITY OF THE RIGHTEOUS

When the godly remember their eternal citizenship in heaven but also assume their responsibility as citizens on earth, entire cities and nations prosper (11:10, 14). Paul instructs us not only to respect and obey governing authorities but also to be ready to do what is good (Titus 3:1). As we take our rightful place in American democracy, Paul cautions us to avoid slander and to be "peaceable," "considerate," and "humble toward all men" (Titus 3:2). We must remember that the only lasting solution to the human condition of slavery to immoral passions is not better laws or social programs but the forgiveness and renewal that only the crucified, resurrected Savior can give (Titus 3:3-8). Opportunities to tell this truth come when we get involved in a community, not when we withdraw.

Today in the mail I received a Safe Homes Directory for our town. In response to the many unsupervised parties where drugs and alcohol are the main ingredients for the destruction of lives and property, some citizens banded together and encouraged parents to sign the following pledge:

I Pledge to Provide a Safe Home

- I will not allow parties or gatherings in my home when I'm not there.
- I will not serve nor will I allow youth under the drinking age to consume alcohol in my home or on my property.
- I will not allow the use of illegal drugs in my home or on my property.

The cover letter accompanying the directory closed with these words: "The key to the Safe Homes Program is for you to realize *you are not alone* in your ideal to have an alcohol/drug free community. Use the directory to meet people who have publicly taken a firm stand of non-tolerance and non-acceptance of alcohol /drug use by our young people in our community. Just think of the impact it would make on Midlothian if each of you encourages just one more family to sign the pledge! You can make a difference." The letter is signed Barbara Jackson, Chairman Safe Homes Project. Barb also directs our children's church on Sunday morning.

The Safe Homes Project was sponsored by REACH (Resources-Education-Action-Council-Helping). When George Raffield, a young undercover officer, was murdered by some high school students in a field a few miles from our church, Vera Wofford, another member of our church family, decided to unite the resources of our town against illicit drugs and alcohol abuse. And REACH was born.

Jacci Vitovsky and her husband, Ed, head up a group of kindergarten through second grade kids, the AWANA Sparks, every Wednesday. Jacci also leads the singing for the children before they go to their individual Sunday school classes on Sunday morning. These activities did not blind her to the need for first graders in our public school to increase their literacy skills. She came up with the idea of getting dads to volunteer about an hour a week to come to the elementary school and listen to a first grader read aloud for fifteen minutes. Sixteen dads volunteered, and the children were chosen at random until everyone had his or her turn. The teacher drew the first name, and the child went for the special time of reading. At the end of the session the volunteer dad came to the teacher with moist eyes. The child had never been able to read to a dad. He had never seen his own daddy. Jacci recently received a letter of commendation from Barbara Bush for her efforts in literacy and involving dads with kids.

These believers did not compromise with the world but are penetrating the world for Christ. We are to separate ourselves from the world of evil—all that is hostile to God and His moral standards—but we must not separate ourselves from the world of people. Jesus loves this world.

Conclusion

Our children grow up and cease to be children. This is tough on parents, but if we are wise, we won't resist their growth towards independence. When our kids walk out of childhood into adulthood, two women wait for them on the street—Lady Wisdom and Lady Folly. Proverbs 9 pictures this main street.

Lady Wisdom, as we have learned, seeks to turn hearts toward God and His skillful principles of living. Earlier, she invited the naive teenager to fall in love with her and turn away from the demolition crew with its mocking, dullness, and impenetrability to spiritual values. She challenged the youth to reject self-destructive arrogance and humbly open his ears to her lectures regarding commitment to the Architect and His views concerning money, sex, and power.

When the constraining net of parental authority slips away, it is time for our kids to reveal whether Lady Wisdom has won their hearts. In her home there is warm fellowship with other men and women who have chosen the truth. Jesus promises that this fellowship will never end. It is an invitation to the eternal marriage supper of the Lamb (Proverbs 9:3-5; Revelation 19:9).

In a flaming, seductive red dress Lady Folly waits for our young adults as well. She loves those without a heart—without a godly, moral core. She promises incredible "highs" as her victims enjoy the release from "God's limiting restrictions." Forbidden fruit is the sweetest, she claims. Her home presents itself as a mansion full of delights, but it is all a deceptive facade. Her invitation is to a funeral, not a wedding. When you accept, you enter a morgue, a funeral parlor filled with the corpses of those she has already destroyed.

As parents we cannot control the choices our children will make. We can, however, commit the core of our being to wisdom, illustrate the fruit of this commitment with our life example, and teach our children the facts of life. When it's time for them to walk down Main Street by themselves, we must allow them to decide whether they will enter the house of wisdom or of folly.

> The foolish man built his house upon the sand.
> The foolish man built his house upon the sand.
> The foolish man built his house upon the sand,
> and the rains came tumbling down.
> The rains came down and the flood came up.
> The rains came down and the flood came up.
> The rains came down and the flood came up.
> And the house on the sand went—smash!
>
> The wise man built his house upon the Rock.
> The wise man built his house upon the Rock.
> The wise man built his house upon the Rock,
> and the rains came tumbling down.
> The rains came down and the floods came up.
> The rains came down and the floods came up.
> The rains came down and the floods came up.
> But the house on the Rock stood firm.

(Author unknown)